The Mealthy MultiPot Cookbook for Beginners

Fresh and Foolproof Recipes for
Your Mealthy MultiPot Pressure Cooker

Ashton Mills

Warning-Disclaimer

The purpose of this book is to educate and entertain. The author or publisher does not guarantee that anyone following the techniques, suggestions, tInstant Pots, ideas, or strategies will become successful. The author and publisher shall have neither liability or responsibility to anyone with respect to any loss or damage caused, or alleged to be caused, directly or indirectly by the information contained in this book.

CONTENTS

Poultry Recipes 39

Red Meat Recipes.. 51

Seafood Recipes.. 67

INTRODUCTION

Pressure cookers offer an efficient, time-saving, and effortless way to enjoy a delicious meal without sacrificing the wonderful taste. But what was every housewife's favorite kitchen appliance in the 1950s has surely evolved into a powerful and much more convenient tool that every kitchen should be equipped with.

Electric pressure cookers may have been around since 1991, but it wasn't until recently that they really reached their peak. There are many electric pressure cookers currently on the market – all with smart programming and the most satisfying options – however, there is one pressure cooker in particular that stands out and casts a shadow on its competitors. The most versatile electric pressure cooker that you can currently buy is, beyond doubt, the Mealthy MultiPot Multi-Cooker.

Whether you already own one and are looking for some yummy recipes for your Mealthy MultiPot Pressure Cooker, or you need a little nudge that will convince you to buy one, one thing is for sure: this book will definitely help you prepare effortless and delicious meals.

Inside this book you will not only find over a hundred decadent and absolutely irresistible recipes, all with nutritional facts, to satisfy everyone, but you will also learn what makes the Mealthy MultiPot Multi-Cooker so powerful and why it is worth your buck.

It may cook with pressure, but the Mealthy MultiPot will never leave you under pressure while cooking.

Mealthy MultiPot Multi-Cooker – The Revolutionary Cooking Appliance

If you think that there is no way for you to whip up delicious, nutritious, and super flavorful meals with a single touch of a button, then you better think again because Mealthy MultiPot Multi-Cooker is about to become the definition of quick, effortless, and healthy cooking.

THE BENEFITS

So, why should you buy the Mealthy MultiPot Pressure Cooker? Besides the fact that the Mealthy MultiPot Multi-Cooker has an incredible build quality and flavor infusion technology, here are some other benefits that will convince you why setting some money aside for this dream-come-true appliance of every homemaker is the best home investment to make this very instant:

It Saves Energy

Pressure cookers require less time to prepare food, which means that they use less energy to create equally delicious meals. Say goodbye to wasting your energy with your pots, pans, and burners, because once you start cooking with the Mealthy Pressure Cooker, you will drastically cut back on energy. That will not only keep more money in your pocket each month, but it will also keep your stove clean at all times – since you will rarely use it.

It is Super Time Efficient

The Mealthy MultiPot Multi-Cooker traps the heated steam that occurs inside the pot during the process of cooking and creates a high-pressure environment that contributes to quick cooking. But besides the fact that the steam and pressure will cook your meals 70 % faster than your stove, the efficiency of the Mealthy MultiPot is also in the preparation method. Because it requires no other pans, skillets, or woks, and uses a single-pot cooking method, the Mealthy MultiPot requires no special preparations, cooks without too much hassle, and will help you serve delicious meals in a snap.

It is Economical

Not only will the Mealthy MultiPot Multi-Cooker save you time and money from energy, but it will also allow you to cook inexpensive food to such a juicy and delightful perfection as if you used the most expensive cuts of meat and not those chops that were on sale.

It Preserves the Nutrients

Unlike the meals cooked with most of the traditional cookware, the Mealthy MultiPot Multi-Cooker leaves the nutrients intact. Due to the steam and pressure flow that is going on inside the Mealthy MultiPot during the cooking process, the food preserves its moisture and juiciness even after being cooked. The high-pressure environment locks inside all of the precious vitamins and nutrients, which adds healthier and more nutritious meals to your dinner table.

It Does Not Expose You to Harmful Substances

It is not uncommon for most cooking methods to deprive the foods of their wholesomeness and destroy the vitamins, minerals and other nutrients during the process of cooking, but they also create certain harmful compounds such as elements that can cause cancer or elevate the blood pressure. This is yet another reason why you should choose to cook your meals with the Mealthy MultiPot. When cooked under pressure, the food preserves its nutrients and does not get exposed to harmful compounds.

It Has a Canning Option

Unlike many other pressure cookers, this amazing kitchen appliance comes with the option for canning and preserving food. If you love using those extra fruits and veggies for creating some yummy canned good, then this is definitely the way to do it.

THE BUTTONS

If you are a proud owner of a new and shiny Mealthy MultiPot Multi-Cooker, you may be a little bit intimidated by the number of buttons found on the front of the cooker. Do not let its multi-functionality overwhelm you. The buttons aren't there to be overwhelming but to actually to make the cooking experience a lot more convenient for you. Once you start cooking and really 'feel' how every button works, I promise you; you won't even think about turning on your stove.

Here are the Mealthy MultiPot Multi-Cooker buttons and how to use them:

Sauté – This button starts the cooking process after selecting on which setting you want to cook. Use it for sautéing onion, garlic or to sear the meat. Cook with the lid off.

Start/Delay – This button starts the cooking process after selecting on which setting you want to cook. Press it to stop the cooking process and/or change the cooking settings. Please use as directed on your Mealthy MultiPot Multi-Cooker manual.

Delay Timer – This magical little option actually allows you to delay the cooking process. That means that you can set your pressure cooker for later in the day. For instance, if you want to have a warm dinner waiting for you when you get home from work, all you have to do is simply whip up the meal, place it inside the Mealthy MultiPot Multi-Cooker, and enter when you want it to start cooking. Amazing, right?

Soup/Broth – This option for making soups and stews has a recommended setting for a cooking time of 15 to 25 minutes. That means that if you press this button, it will pressure cook your food for 20 minutes only. However, this button also allows you to use the cook time selector and adjust the cooking time according to your desire.

Slow Cook – Although this is a pressure cooker, the Mealthy MultiPot Multi-Cooker can also replace a slow cooker as well. If you want to slow cook a meal, all you have to do is choose the "slow cook" option.

Rice – The Mealthy MultiPot Multi-Cooker recommends that, if you are cooking rice, you do it with this option.

Beans/Chili – If you are making chili, or cooking beans, lentils, or similar meals, you can easily do it with this option.

Poultry – Since the Mealthy MultiPot Multi-Cooker does not have a 'manual' button such as the Instant Pot, I find this one to be a pretty good manual replacement and the one you should use when cooking chicken or turkey.

Meat/Stew – Excellent for beef and stews. It cooks the meals perfectly, and you will enjoy this setting a lot.

Keep/Warm – this option keeps your meals fresh and warm until you are ready to serve.

Multigrain – this option is perfect for cooking grains.

Porridge – this option essentially turns your Mealthy MultiPot Multi-Cooker into a porridge maker.

Cake – this option allows you to prepare delicious desserts, however not all desserts are prepared using this function.

Steam – this option allows you to prepare delicious fish or steam vegetables

Egg – this option allows you to make delightful egg meals or just your favorite boiled eggs

COOKING TIPS

The Mealthy MultiPot Multi-Cooker is not your regular kitchen appliance. It is in fact so versatile and multi-functional, and is a combination of many other appliances:
- It is a pressure cooker
- It is a slow cooker
- It is a sautéing pan and a stove top
- It is a rice cooker
- It is a steamer
- It is a warming pot
- It is a yogurt maker

If you have all of these appliances crowding your kitchen, replacing some of them with the Mealthy MultiPot Multi-Cooker is definitely the best choice.

However, it is its very versatility that intimidates people. If you are one of the many that simply cannot figure out how to get the most out of this device, then you might want to pay attention to these net revolutionary tips:

— You can cook frozen food without defrosting. All you have to do is simply add a couple of minutes to your cooking time.

— Do not force open the lid. You must allow for the pressure to be fully released before opening the lid. If the lid doesn't open, don't worry, it isn't stuck. That is just an indication that the Mealthy MultiPot pressure cooker is still pressurized and it still isn't safe to open the lid. Allow a few more minutes and try again.

— The Mealthy MultiPot pressure cooker is extremely safe to use, but only if you use it right. The best way to ensure that you will stay safe during releasing pressure and opening the lid is by ensuring that the venting knob is turned to the venting position, and by tilting the lid away from you when opening.

— The Mealthy MultiPot pressure cooker does not have a sautéing or browning function. With this appliance, you can easily sauté food by choosing any of the given cooking options and cooking with the lid open. This makes the Mealthy MultiPot pressure cooker even more functional.

— Make sure not to overfill the Mealthy MultiPot Multi-Cooker. This will only increase the pressure and may even clog the valve. For best results, fill your Mealthy MultiPot Multi-Cooker up until it is 2/3 full. However, if you are cooking food that may raise or expand during the cooking process, fill it only halfway.

— Do not use too much liquid. Always follow the recipes until you have some experience under your belt and can create delicious recipes on your own. If you add more liquid than necessary, this will not only give your meals that 'rinsed' taste and dilute them, but it will also increase the time that is needed for the Mealthy MultiPot Multi-Cooker to go to pressure.

THE PRESSURE RELEASE

Luckily for every new user, the pressure valve of the Mealthy MultiPot Multi-Cooker has some pretty visible and easy-to-figure-out signs. If you line up the circle symbol, you will lock the pressure in, and if you line up the symbol of the steam coming out, you are about to release the pressure.

Now, as to when you should use the quick release or natural pressure release method, here is what you should know.

Quick – The quick pressure release method means allowing the steam to come out quickly. There really isn't a rule, and you can basically use this method anytime; however, you do have to keep in mind that if the Mealthy MultiPot Multi-Cooker is filled with liquid and you release the steam out quickly, spillage will most likely occur. This method is best to use after cooking meat, seafood, or veggies.

Natural – The natural pressure release method means just the opposite – allowing the steam to come out slowly. This method is best after cooking content that is starch-high, foamy food, or food with a large liquid volume.

THE COOKING TIME

It would be remiss not to mention this, I know, but since there is pretty detailed information about the cooking time found in your Mealthy MultiPot Multi-Cooker manual, I will briefly explain the basis.

Here is how long you should cook food in your Mealthy MultiPot Multi-Cooker:
- Fresh Fish– ready after 2-5 minutes of cooking
- Vegetables – ready after 2-5 minutes of cooking
- Chili – usual cooking time is 30 minutes
- Beef Roast – usual cooking time is 35 – 40 minutes
- Pork Roast – usual cooking time is 40 – 45 minutes
- Whole Chicken – usual cooking time is 20 minutes
- Juicy Ribs – usual cooking time is 20 minutes

BREAKFAST RECIPES

Arugula Mozarella Eggs with Hollandaise Sauce

Preparation Time: 12 minutes / Servings: 4

Nutrition Facts

Per Serving: Calories 314, Carbs 12.9 g, Fiber 0.1 g, Fat 20.6 g, Protein 19.4 g

Ingredients

4 Bread Slices, chopped

4 Eggs, whisked

½ cup Arugula, chopped

4 slices of Mozzarella Cheese

1 cup Water

1 ½ ounces Hollandaise Sauce

How To

1. Insert the steamer basket in your pressure cooker and pour the water inside.
2. Place the bread pieces in 4 ramekins.
3. Combine the eggs and arugula and divide this mixture between the ramekins.
4. Cover them with aluminum foil and close the lid of your pressure cooker.
5. Cook on High pressure for 5 minutes on PRESSURE COOK.
6. Once cooking is complete, do a quick pressure release.
7. Discard the foil and top with a slice of mozzarella and the hollandaise sauce.
8. Enjoy.

Savory Cremini Oatmeal

Preparation Time: 30 minutes / Servings: 4

Nutrition Facts

Per Serving: Calories 451, Carbs 61 g, Fiber 5 g, Fat 15 g, Protein 29 g

Ingredients

8 ounces Cremini Mushrooms, sliced

14 ounces Chicken Broth

½ Onion, diced

2 tbsp Butter

1 cup Steel-Cut Oats

½ cup grated Gouda Cheese

3 sprigs Thyme, chopped

½ cup Water

1 Garlic Clove, minced

Kosher Salt and Black Pepper, to taste

How To

1. Preheat the pressure cooker by selecting SAUTÉ. Add the butter and melt it. Once melted, add the onion and mushrooms and sauté for 3 minutes, until tender.
2. Add garlic and cook for one more minute.
3. Stir in the oats and cook for an additional minute.
4. Pour in the water, broth, and add thyme sprigs. Season with salt and pepper.
5. Secure the lid, and select PRESSURE COOK. Cook for 12 minutes on High pressure.
6. Once cooking is complete, allow pressure to release naturally for 10 minutes then turn the pressure valve to release any remaining pressure.
7. Serve the oatmeal topped with Gouda Cheese.

No Crust Three-Meat Quiche

Preparation Time: 50 minutes / Servings: 4

Nutrition Facts

Per Serving: Calories 424, Carbs 6.3 g, Fiber 0.3 g, Fat 31.9 g, Protein 31.8 g

Ingredients

6 Eggs, beaten

1 cup cooked Ground Sausage

4 Bacon slices, cooked and crumbled

2 Green Onions, chopped

½ cup Milk

4 Ham Slices, diced

1 ½ cups Water

1 cup grated Cheddar, plus more as desired

¼ tsp Salt

Pinch of Black Pepper

How To

1. Put the trivet inside the pressure cooker and pour the water in.
2. Make a sling with foil so you can remove the baking dish easily when it's ready.
3. In a large bowl, whisk together the eggs, milk, salt, and pepper until well mixed.
4. Combine the sausage, cheese, bacon, ham, and onions in a baking dish.
5. Pour the egg mixture over. Lower the dish onto the trivet; cover with aluminum foil and secure the lid.
6. Select PRESSURE COOK and cook for about 30 minutes on High pressure.
7. When cooking is complete, perform a quick pressure release, then turn the pressure valve to release any remaining pressure.
8. Carefully open the lid, take out the dish and remove the foil. Serve immediately.

Crispy Bacon and Egg Sandwich

Preparation Time: 22 minutes / Servings: 1

Nutrition Facts

Per Serving: Calories 488, Carbs 37 g, Fiber 3.1 g, Fat 33 g, Protein 20 g

Ingredients

2 slices of Bread

1 Egg

2 Slices of bacon

1 tsp Olive Oil

1 tbsp grated Cheese by choice

1 cup Water

How To

1. Heat olive oil in the pressure cooker by choosing SAUTÉ option.
2. Add the bacon and cook until crispy. Transfer to a plate, shred and take a paper towel to wipe out the excess grease.
3. Add the water to the pressure cooker.
4. Crumble the bacon in a ramekin, and crack the egg on top.
5. Sprinkle the egg with cheese.
6. Cap the ramekin with aluminum foil and place it on top of the trivet inside the pressure cooker.
7. Secure the lid and cook for 6 minutes on MEAT/STEW mode on High Pressure.
8. Once cooking is complete, wait for 10 minutes to do a quick pressure release.
9. Carefully open the lid.
10. Assemble the sandwich and enjoy.

Easy Citrusy French Toast

Preparation Time: 35 minutes / Servings: 4

Nutrition Facts

Per Serving: Calories 315, Carbs 44.4 g, Fiber 3.4 g, Fat 15.2 g, Protein 14.6 g

Ingredients

Zest of 1 Orange

1 cup Water

¼ cup Granulated Sugar

2 large Eggs

3 tbsp Butter, melted

1 ¼ cups Milk

½ tsp Vanilla Extract

1 loaf of Challah Bread, cut into pieces

Pinch of Sea Salt

How To

1. Whisk together all of the ingredients, except the water and bread, in a large bowl.
2. Place the bread in the bowl and coat it well in the mixture.
3. Arrange the coated bread pieces in a baking dish.
4. Gently put the trivet in your pressure cooker. Pour the water inside.
5. Lower the baking dish onto the trivet. Then, secure the lid.
6. Select PRESSURE COOK and cook for 25 minutes on High pressure.
7. Once cooking is completed, allow the pressure to release naturally for 15 minutes.
8. Carefully remove the baking dish using oven tongs.
9. Serve immediately.

Tasty Sweet Potato Frittata

Preparation Time: 28 minutes / Servings: 4

Nutrition Facts

Per Serving: Calories 168, Carbs 11.8 g, Fiber 1.6 g, Fat 11.3 g, Protein 5.9 g

Ingredients

6 large Eggs, beaten

1 Tomato, chopped

¼ cup Almond Milk

1 tbsp Tomato Paste

1 tbsp Olive Oil

2 tbsp Coconut Flour

1 ½ cups Water

5 tbsp chopped Onion

1 tsp minced Garlic Clove

4 ounces shredded Sweet Potatoes

Fresh basil, for garnish

How To

1. Whisk the wet ingredients together in a bowl, excluding the water.
2. Fold in the dry ingredients and stir to combine well.
3. Pour the mixture into a greased baking dish.
4. Place a trivet in the pressure cooker and pour the water inside.
5. Insert the baking dish in your pressure cooker and close the lid.
6. Select PRESSURE COOK and cook for 18 minutes on High pressure.
7. Once the cooking cycle has finished, allow pressure to release naturally for 10 minutes.
8. Carefully remove the baking dish and serve topped with fresh basil.

Spanish Chorizo and Kale Egg Casserole

Preparation Time: 40 minutes / Servings: 4 / Servings: 4

Nutrition Facts

Per Serving: Calories 523, Carbs 13.2 g, Fiber 1.6 g, Fat 30.2 g, Protein 34.3 g

Ingredients

8 ounces Chorizo, cooked

1 tbsp Coconut Oil

6 Eggs

¾ cup sliced Leek

1 ½ cups Water

1 cup Kale, chopped

1 Sweet Potato, shredded

1 tsp minced Garlic

How To

1. Melt the coconut oil in your pressure cooker by pressing SAUTÉ.
2. Add garlic, kale, and leeks, and cook them for a couple of minutes, until soft.
3. Meanwhile, grease a baking dish.
4. Place the veggies in the baking dish.
5. In a separate bowl, beat the eggs and pour them over the veggies.
6. Stir in chorizo and sweet potato.
7. Place the trivet in your pressure cooker and pour the water inside.
8. Place the baking dish inside the pressure cooker, close the lid, and cook on MEAT/STEW for about 25 minutes on High pressure.
9. Once the cooking cycle has stopped, do a quick pressure release.
10. Cut into slices and serve.

Blackberries Quinoa Breakfast Bowl

Preparation Time: 13-15 minutes / Servings: 4

Nutrition Facts

Per Serving: Calories 242, Carbs 45.7 g, Fiber 3 g, Fat 2.5 g, Protein 6.4 g

Ingredients

1 cup Quinoa, rinsed and drained

2 tbsp Maple Syrup

1 tsp Vanilla Extract

1 cup blueberries

1 ½ cups Water

A pinch of Sea Salt

How To

1. Add the quinoa, water, vanilla extract, maple syrup, and salt to the pressure cooker. Stir to combine well.
2. Seal the lid. Select PRESSURE COOK button and cook on High Pressure for 10 minutes.
3. Once cooking is complete, wait for 10 minutes to do a quick pressure release.
4. Fluff with a fork. Serve in four bowls topped with the blackberries.

Cheddar, Ham, and Eggs Hash Bake

Preparation Time: 11 minutes / Servings: 4

Nutrition Facts

Per Serving: Calories 587, Carbs 98 g, Fiber 16.1 g, Fat 12.3 g, Protein 26.8 g

Ingredients

6 small Potatoes, shredded

6 large Eggs, beaten

¼ cup Water

1 cup Cheddar Cheese, shredded

1 cup Ham, diced

How To

1. Spray the interior of a pressure cooker with nonstick cooking spray. Turn the pressure cooker on just to preheat it.
2. Place the shredded potatoes inside and cook on SAUTÉ mode until slightly browned, for about 10 minutes. Stir in the water.
3. In a bowl, mix the ham, cheese, and eggs, and transfer this mixture to the pressure cooker. Stir to combine well. Secure the lid and set the valve to Sealing.
4. Press PRESSURE COOK button and adjust cooking time to 5 minutes on High Pressure.
5. Once cooking is completed, perform a quick pressure release. Serve immediately

Quick Cherry and Chocolate Oatmeal

Preparation Time: 15 minutes / Servings:4

Nutrition Facts

Per Serving: Calories 187, Carbs 34 g, Fiber 5.6 g, Fat 4.6 g, Protein 5.1 g

Ingredients

3 ½ cups Water

2 tbsp Sugar

1 cup Steel-Cut Oats

3 tbsp Dark Chocolate Chips

1 cup Frozen Cherries, pitted

A pinch of Sea Salt

How To

1. Place all of the ingredients except the chocolate in your pressure cooker.
2. Stir well to combine. Close the lid.
3. Select the POULTRY mode and cook for 12 minutes on High pressure.
4. When the timer beeps, perform a quick pressure release. Stir in chocolate chips and serve immediately.

Cinnamon French Toast with Banana

Preparation Time: 50 minutes / Servings: 6

Nutrition Facts

Per Serving: Calories 313, Carbs 39 g, Fiber 2 g, Fat 15 g, Protein 8 g

Ingredients

1 ½ tsp Cinnamon

¼ tsp Vanilla Extract

6 Bread Slices, cubed

4 Bananas, sliced

2 tbsp Brown Sugar

1 tbsp White Sugar

½ cup Milk

¼ cup Pecans, chopped

3 Eggs

¼ cup Cream Cheese, softened

2 tbsp cold and sliced Butter

¾ cup Water

How To

1. Grease a 1 ½ - quart baking dish and arrange half of the bread cubes.
2. Top the bread with half of the banana slices.
3. Sprinkle half of the brown sugar over.
4. Spread the cream cheese over the bananas.
5. Arrange the rest of the bread cubes and banana slices over.
6. Sprinkle with the remaining brown sugar and pecans.
7. Top with the butter slices.
8. Whisk together the eggs, white sugar, milk, cinnamon, and vanilla in a bowl.
9. Pour the mixture over.
10. Place the trivet inside the pressure cooker and add the water.
11. Lower the baking dish on the trivet, seal the lid and cook on PRESSURE COOK for 30 minutes on High pressure.
12. Once cooking is complete, release the pressure quickly.
13. Place French toast on plates. Top with remaining banana slices. Serve and enjoy.

Giant Coconut Pancake

Preparation Time: 55 minutes / Servings: 4

Nutrition Facts

Per Serving: Calories 358, Carbs 39 g, Fiber 18 g, Fat 18.3 g, Protein 8.1 g

Ingredients

1 cup Coconut Flour

1 tsp Coconut Extract

2 tbsp Honey

2 Eggs

1 ½ cups Coconut Milk

1 cup ground Almonds

½ tsp Baking Soda

1 tablespoon coconut butter, melted, divided

How To

1. Whisk together the eggs and milk in a bowl until completely combined.
2. Add the other ingredients gradually, while constantly whisking.
3. Lightly butter the interior of your MultiPot with coconut butter. Pour in batter
4. Seal the lid and set the steam vent to Sealing.
5. Select PRESSURE COOK and cook for 45 minutes on Low pressure.
6. Once the time is up, use a natural release for 10 minutes, then turn the pressure valve to release any remaining pressure.
7. Transfer the pancake to a plate, and serve with your favorite pancake toppings.

SOUPS AND STEWS

Quick Ham and Peas Soup

Preparation Time: 40 minutes / Servings: 4

Nutrition Facts

Per Serving: Calories 276, Carbs 15.9 g, Fiber 20.5 g, Fat 10 g, Protein 29.1 g

Ingredients

1 Onion, diced

1 pound Split Peas, dried

2 Carrots, diced

6 cups vegetable stock

2 Celery Stalks, diced

1 pound Ham Chunks

1 ½ tsp dried Thyme

1 tablespoon olive oil

How To

1. Heat oil in the pressure cooker on SAUTÉ mode.
2. Add the onion, carrots, and celery and cook until soft, about 3 minutes.
3. Stir ham chunks, broth, split peas, and dried thyme with the vegetables.
4. Lock the lid in place and set the steam vent to Sealing.
5. Press Soup/Broth button and cook for 20 minutes on High pressure.
6. Once the cooking cycle has completed, perform a quick pressure release.
7. Serve hot and enjoy.

Penne Minestrone Soup

Preparation Time: 15 minutes / Servings:6

Nutrition Facts

Per Serving: Calories 167, Carbs 18.2 g, Fiber 4.3 g, Fat 6.1 g, Protein 10.4 g

Ingredients

1 Onion, diced

2 Carrots, diced

1 tbsp minced Garlic

2 tbsp Olive Oil

4 cups Veggie Broth

24 ounces jarred Spaghetti Sauce

1 tsp Sugar

2 Celery Stalks, sliced

¼ tsp Black Pepper

1 ½ tsp Italian Seasoning

14 ounces canned diced Tomatoes

8 ounces dry Cheese Penne

Basil sprigs, to garnish (optional)

How To

1. To preheat the MultiPot, select SAUTÉ. Add the olive oil, onions, garlic, celery, and carrots, and cook until they start to 'sweat', about 6 minutes. Stir in the rest of the ingredients. Secure the lid.

2. Select PRESSURE COOK BUTTON and cook on high pressure for 10 minutes, then turn the pressure valve to release any remaining pressure.

3. Once cooking is complete, do a quick pressure release.

4. Check the pasta. If it's too 'al dente' for your liking, you can continue boiling them with the lid off for a few more minutes. Taste for seasoning.

5. Serve immediately. Garnish with basil, if desired.

Button Mushroom and Beef Stew

Preparation Time: 30 minutes / Servings: 6

Nutrition Facts

Per Serving: Calories 450, Carbs 43 g, Fiber 6.3 g, Fat 15.7 g, Protein 36.6 g

Ingredients

2 tbsp Canola Oil

1 tsp dried Parsley

1 Onion, chopped

1 ½ pound Beef, cut into pieces

4 Red Potatoes, cut into chunks

4 Carrots, cut into chunks

8 Button Mushrooms, sliced

10 ounces Golden Mushroom Soup

12 ounces Water

1 celery stalk, chopped

1 bay leaf

Salt and freshly ground pepper, to taste

Chopped fresh parsley to taste

How To

1. Heat the oil in the pressure cooker by setting SAUTÉ. Add the onion, carrots, and celery and cook for 3 minutes until they are tender and aromatic.
2. Add the beef and brown it on all sides for 7 to 8 minutes.
3. Stir in the remaining ingredients. Seal the lid.
4. Select Meat/Stew mode and cook on High Pressure for 20 minutes.
5. Once cooking is complete, allow for a natural release for 10 minutes.
6. Remove and discard the bay leaf. Season with salt and pepper. Serve in bowls garnished with fresh parsley.

Delicious Chicken Enchilada Soup

Preparation Time: 40 minutes / Servings: 6

Nutrition Facts

Per Serving: Calories 553, Carbs 56 g, Fiber 3 g, Fat 15 g, Protein 62 g

Ingredients

8 cups cubed Butternut Squash

1 pound boneless and skinless Chicken Breasts

1 can (10 ounces) Enchilada sauce

2 tsp Cumin

2 tsp olive oil

1 Onion, chopped

3 ½ ounces canned chopped Chillies

2 tsp Taco Seasoning

3 Russet Potatoes, quartered

2 Garlic Cloves, minced

4 cups Chicken Broth

1 (15.5 ounces) can Cannellini Beans, rinsed and drained

1 Red Bell Pepper, chopped

How To

1. Heat the oil in the pressure cooker by setting to Sauté. Add the onion and cook for 3 minutes until tender. Add the remaining ingredients and stir to combine well. Seal the lid.
2. Select SOUP/BROTH and cook on High pressure for 24 minutes.
3. Once the cooking cycle has terminated, allow pressure to release naturally for 10 minutes, turn the pressure valve to release any remaining pressure.
4. Remove the chicken from the cooker. Using a hand blender, blend the soup until smooth. Shred the chicken with two forks and return the meat to the soup.

Classic Lentil Soup

Preparation Time: 40 minutes / Servings: 4

Nutrition Facts

Per Serving: Calories 145, Carbs 10.4 g, Fiber 1.3 g, Fat 7.5 g, Protein 7.3 g

Ingredients

2 Garlic Cloves, minced

1 tsp Cumin

4 cups Veggie Broth

½ Onion, chopped

2 Celery Stalks, chopped

1 Carrot, chopped

1 cup dry Lentils

1 Bay Leaf

2 tbsp Olive Oil

Salt and Pepper, to taste

Fresh cilantro for garnish

How To

1. Heat olive oil in your pressure cooker set to SAUTÉ.
2. Add onions, garlic, carrots, and celery and cook until they start to 'sweat', about 5 minutes. Stir in the remaining ingredients. Seal the lid.
3. Select SOUP/BROTH and cook for 20 minutes on High pressure.
4. Once the cooking cycle has finished, allow pressure to release naturally for 10 minutes; turn the pressure valve to release any remaining pressure.
5. Taste and adjust the seasonings. Afterwards, ladle lentil soup into bowls; drizzle with fresh cilantro and serve right away!

Gaelic Lamb Stew

Preparation Time: 40 minutes / Servings: 4

Nutrition Facts

Per Serving: Calories 451, Carbs 25.8 g, Fiber 3.9 g, Fat 21.4 g, Protein 34.8 g

Ingredients

1 pound Lamb, cut into pieces

1 Onion, sliced

2 tbsp Cornstarch

1 ½ tbsp Olive Oil

2 Sweet Potatoes, cut into cubes

3 Carrots, chopped

2 ½ cups Veggie Broth

½ tsp dried Thyme

Fresh parsley sprigs for garnish

How To

1. Heat olive oil in your pressure cooker set to SAUTÉ.
2. Add the lamb and cook until browned on all sides, about 6 minutes.
3. Add all of the remaining ingredients, except the cornstarch, and stir well to combine. Lock the lid in place.
4. Select PRESSURE COOK and cook for 10 minutes on High pressure.
5. Once ready, let the pressure release naturally for 15 minutes, then turn the pressure valve to release any remaining pressure.
6. Whisk the cornstarch with a little bit of water and stir in a bowl to dissolve cornstarch completely; pour into the stew and mix well.
7. Cook on 2-3 more minutes without the lid until desired thickness is reached, 5 to 6 minutes.
8. Serve sprinkled with fresh parsley.

Savory Navy Bean and Ham Shank Soup

Preparation Time: 8 hours and 30 minutes / Servings: 12

Nutrition Facts

Per Serving: Calories 471, Carbs 48.7 g, Fiber 13.9 g, Fat 14 g, Protein 36 g

Ingredients

½ cup Vegetable Oil

4 cups dried Navy Beans

3 pounds Ham Shank

2 Onions, chopped

4 Carrots, sliced

½ cup minced Green Pepper

3 Quarts Water

2 cups Tomato Sauce

4 Celery Stalks, chopped

2 Garlic Cloves, minced

Salt and Pepper, to taste

2 tbsp chopped fresh parsley leaves

How To

1. Soak the beans in the vegetable oil with some salt and pepper overnight. Drain them well.
2. Heat the oil in your pressure cooker set to SAUTÉ. Add onions and cook for 3 minutes. Stir in the beans and the remaining ingredients. Stir well to combine. Seal the lid.
3. Place the beans in the Multi-Pot and add all of the remaining ingredients.
4. Select SOUP/BROTH and cook for 25 minutes on Hgh pressure.
5. Once the cooking cycle has completed, release the pressure naturally for 10 minutes, then turn the pressure valve to release any remaining pressure.
6. Top with parsley and serve.

Skim and Fast Miso and Tofu Soup

Preparation Time: 12 minutes / Servings: 4

Nutrition Facts

Per Serving: Calories 146, Carbs 31.7 g, Fiber 1 g, Fat 2.7 g, Protein 5.8 g

Ingredients

4 cups Water

½ cup Corn

2 tbsp Miso Paste

1 Onion, sliced

1 tsp Wakame Flakes

1 cup Silken Tofu, cubed

2 Celery Stalks, chopped

2 Carrots, chopped

Soy Sauce, to taste

How To

1. Combine corn, onion, wakame flakes, carrots, water, and celery in your MultiPot pressure cooker.
2. Seal the lid. Select SOUP/BROTH and cook for 10 minutes on High pressure.
3. Once cooking is complete, release the pressure quickly.
4. In a small bowl mix the miso paste with one cup of the broth and stir to combine; pour into the soup.
5. Add tofu and some soy sauce and stir.
6. Taste and add some salt if desired.
7. Serve warm and enjoy.

Italian-Style Tomato Soup

Preparation Time: 25 minutes / Servings: 8

Nutrition Facts

Per Serving: Calories 314, Carbs 16 g, Fiber 2 g, Fat 23 g, Protein 11 g

Ingredients

3 pounds Tomatoes, peeled and quartered

1 Carrot, diced

1 Onion, diced

¼ cup chopped Fresh Basil

1 cup heavy cream

1 tbsp Tomato Paste

3 tbsp Butter

½ tsp Salt

½ tsp Pepper

29 ounces Chicken Broth

½ cup grated Parmesan Cheese

1 tsp minced Garlic

How To

1. Melt the butter in your MultiPot by selecting SAUTÉ.
2. Add the onions, celery, and carrots and cook until they start to 'sweat', about 6 minutes. Add garlic and cook for 30 more seconds.
3. Stir in the remaining ingredients, except the cream and cheese. Seal the lid.
4. Select SOUP/BROTH and cook for 10 minutes on High pressure.
5. Press CANCEL and wait for 5 minutes before doing a quick pressure release.
6. Stir in the cream and parmesan cheese.
7. Serve the soup warm!

Beef Chili

Preparation Time: 45 minutes / Servings: 4

Nutrition Facts

Per Serving: Calories 388, Carbs 15.2 g, Fiber 2.9 g, Fat 17.6 g, Protein 22 g

Ingredients

1 pound Ground Beef

½ cup Beef Broth

1 Onion, diced

1 tbsp Olive Oil

28 ounces canned Tomatoes

½ tbsp Cumin

1 ½ tbsp Chili Powder

1 tsp Garlic Powder

2 tbsp Tomato Paste

2 tablespoons chopped fresh parsley leaves

How To

1. Heat the olive oil in your MultiPot by selecting SAUTÉ mode.
2. Add the beef and cook until browned, about 4 minutes.
3. Add the onion and cook for another 2 minutes.
4. Add cumin, chili, garlic powder, tomato paste, and cook for an additional minute.
5. Stir in the tomatoes and beef broth. Seal the lid.
6. Select PRESSURE COOKER mode and cook for 25 minutes on High pressure.
7. Once cooking is complete, do a quick pressure release.
8. Top with parsley and serve.

Pumpkin Chicken Chowder with Corn

Preparation Time: 15 minutes / Servings: 8

Nutrition Facts

Per Serving: Calories 414, Carbs 37 g, Fiber 6 g, Fat 21 g, Protein 41.7 g

Ingredients

2 Chicken Breasts

2 cups Corn, canned or frozen

1 Onion, diced

¼ tsp Pepper

½ cup heavy cream

15 ounces Pumpkin Puree

29 ounces Chicken Broth

½ tsp dried Oregano

1 Garlic Clove, minced

A pinch of Nutmeg

A pinch of Red Pepper Flakes

2 Potatoes, cubed

2 tbsp Butter

2 tbsp fresh parsley leaves, chopped

How To

1. Turn your MultiPot on and choose the SAUTÉ setting. Melt the butter, add the onion and cook it until is translucent, about 4 minutes. Add garlic and cook for an additional minute.
2. Add the pumpkin puree, broth, and all the seasonings.
3. Stir in potatoes and chicken. Seal the lid. Select PRESSURE COOKER mode and cook for 5 minutes on High pressure.
4. Once cooking is complete, do a quick pressure release. Stir in cream and corn.

Lovely Spicy Beef and Potato Soup

Preparation Time: 25 minutes / Servings: 8

Nutrition Facts

Per Serving: Calories 243, Carbs 27 g, Fiber 4.2 g, Fat 9.3 g, Protein 14.7 g

Ingredients

1 pound Ground Beef

4 cups Water

24 ounces Tomato Sauce

2 cups Fresh Corn

2 tsp Salt

4 cups cubed Potatoes

1 Onion, chopped

½ tsp Hot Pepper Sauce

1 ½ tsp Black Pepper

Cooking Spray

How To

1. Spray the interior of a pressure cooker with nonstick cooking spray.
2. Add the beef and cook until browned, about 5 minutes.
3. Add onions and cook for an additional 2 minutes.
4. Stir in the remaining ingredients. Seal the lid.
5. Choose SOUP/BROTH and cook for 10 minutes on High pressure.
6. Once cooking is complete, release the pressure naturally for 10 minutes.
7. Then turn the pressure valve to release any remaining pressure.
8. Serve topped with chopped parsley

Creamy Curry Flavor Cauliflower Soup

Preparation Time: 35 minutes / Servings: 4

Nutrition Facts

Per Serving: Calories 246, Carbs 19.5 g, Fiber 4.1 g, Fat 17.8 g, Protein 6.8 g

Ingredients

1 Cauliflower Head, chopped

1 tbsp Curry Powder

½ tsp Turmeric Powder

1 Sweet Potato, diced

1 Onion, diced

1 Carrot, diced

1 cup Coconut Milk

2 cups Veggie Broth

½ tbsp Coconut Oil

Salt and pepper, to taste

How To

1. Melt the coconut oil in your MultiPot Cooker by setting SAUTÉ.
2. Add onions and carrots and cook for 3 minutes until they are tender.
3. Add the broth, coconut milk, sweet potato, curry and turmeric powder, and cauliflower. Stir to combine well.
4. Lock the lid in place; set the steam vent to Sealing. Choose SOUP/BROTH, and cook for 15 minutes on High pressure.
5. Once cooking is complete, release the pressure naturally for 10 minutes, then turn the pressure valve to release any remaining pressure.
6. Blend with a hand blender until creamy and uniform. Taste the soup to ensure it's well seasoned.
7. Serve and enjoy.

POULTRY RECIPES

Easy Teriyaki Chicken

Preparation Time: 25 minutes / Servings: 8

Nutrition Facts

Per Serving: Calories 352, Carbs 31 g, Fiber 1.2 g, Fat 11.4 g, Protein 30.7 g

Ingredients

1 cup Chicken Broth

1 cup Brown Sugar

2 tbsp ground Ginger

1 tsp Pepper

3 pounds Boneless and Skinless Chicken Thighs

¼ cup Apple Cider Vinegar

1 cup low-sodium Soy Sauce

20 ounces canned Pineapple, crushed

2 tbsp Garlic Powder

2 tbsp toasted sesame seeds

How To

1. Lay the chicken in your pressure cooker.
2. Combine all of the remaining ingredients in a bowl until the sugar dissolves.
3. Pour the mixture over the meat. Lock the lid.
4. Choose the POULTRY option and cook for 20 minutes on High pressure.
5. Once cooking is complete, wait 2 minutes before releasing the pressure quickly.
6. Sprinkle with the sesame seeds and serve.

Hot Paprika Shredded Chicken

Preparation Time: 1 hour / Servings: 4

Nutrition Facts

Per Serving: Calories 307, Carbs 12 g, Fiber 1 g, Fat 10 g, Protein 38.3 g

Ingredients

1 ½ pound boneless and skinless Chicken Breast

2 cups diced Tomatoes

½ tsp Oregano

2 Green Chilies, seeded and chopped

½ tsp Paprika

2 tbsp Coconut Sugar

½ cup Salsa

1 tsp Cumin

2 tbsp Olive Oil

Fresh parsley or dill, chopped, for garnish

How To

1. In a small bowl, combine the oil with the spices and chilies.
2. Rub the chicken breast with the spicy marinade.
3. Place the meat in your pressure cooker. Add the diced tomatoes. Seal the lid.
4. Select POULTRY and cook for 25 minutes on High pressure.
5. Once the time is up, release the pressure naturally for 10 minutes.
6. Use tongs to transfer the chicken to a cutting board and shred it.
7. Return the shredded meat to the MultiPot Cooker. Seal again the lid.
8. Choose the SLOW COOK and cook for 30 more minutes.
9. At the end of the pressure cooking time, let the pressure release naturally for 10 minutes, then turn the pressure valve to release any remaining pressure.
10. Top with the fresh parsley or dill and serve.

Creamy Turkey and Mushrooms

Preparation Time: 40 minutes / Servings: 4

Nutrition Facts

Per Serving: Calories 367, Carbs 5 g, Fiber 1 g, Fat 12 g, Protein 18 g

Ingredients

20 oz Turkey Breasts, boneless and skinless (1 Turkey breast)
6 oz White Button Mushrooms, sliced
3 tbsp chopped Shallots
½ tsp dried Thyme
½ cup dry White Wine
1 cup Chicken Stock
1 Garlic Clove, minced
2 tbsp Olive Oil
3 tbsp Heavy Cream
1 ½ tbsp Cornstarch

How To

1. Tie the turkey breast with a kitchen string horizontally, leaving approximately 2 inches apart. Season the meat with salt and pepper.
2. Heat half of the olive oil in your MultiPot Cooker by selecting SAUTÉ.
3. Add the turkey and brown it for about 3 minutes on each side. Transfer to a plate.
4. Add the remaining oil, shallots, thyme, garlic, and mushrooms and cook until the veggies begin to soften, about 5 minutes.
5. Add white wine and scrape up the brown bits from the bottom.
6. When the alcohol evaporates, return the turkey to the pressure cooker.
7. Close the lid. Select POULTRY and cook for 22 minutes on High pressure.
8. Combine the heavy cream and cornstarch in a small bowl. Once cooking is complete, release the pressure quickly. Stir in the mixture.
9. Bring the sauce to a boil, then turn the cooker off. Slice the turkey in half and serve topped with the creamy mushroom sauce.

Whole Chicken

Preparation Time: 40 minutes / Servings: 4

Nutrition Facts

Per Serving: Calories 376, Carbs 3 g, Fiber 0 g, Fat 23 g, Protein 28.1 g

Ingredients

1 (2 ½ lbs.) Whole Chicken

2 tbsp Olive Oil

1 ½ cups Water

Salt and Pepper, to taste

1 Onion, diced

2 Carrots, peeled and chopped

2 Celery stalks, chopped

2 fresh Thyme sprigs

How To

1. Rinse the chicken and pat dry. Season with salt and pepper.
2. Press SAUTÉ to heat the oil, add the chicken and cook it for 4 minutes or until browned on all sides. Add the onion, carrots, and celery.
3. Stir and cook for 2 minutes more.
4. Add a rack inside your pressure cooker and pour the water.
5. Lower the chicken onto the rack. Lock the lid.
6. Select POULTRY and cook for 25 minutes on High pressure.
7. Once cooking is complete, release the pressure quickly.
8. Carefully remove the lid. Transfer chicken to a cutting board, and carve into large pieces.
9. Sprinkle the chicken with the thyme and pour over the accumulated juices.
10. Serve immediately.

Yummy Turkey and Potatoes in Buffalo Sauce

Preparation Time: 30 minutes / Servings: 4

Nutrition Facts

Per Serving: Calories 377, Carbs 32 g, Fiber 4 g, Fat 15.3 g, Protein 24.7 g

Ingredients

3 tbsp Olive Oil

4 tbsp Buffalo Sauce

1 pound Sweet Potatoes, cut into cubes

1 ½ pounds Turkey Breast, cut into pieces

½ tsp Garlic Powder

1 Onion, diced

2 cups Chicken broth

1 tbsp dried oregano

½ cup Black olives, cut into rings

How To

1. Heat 2 tablespoons of olive oil in your MultiPot pressure cooker on SAUTÉ mode.
2. Add the onion and cook for 3 minutes until is translucent.
3. Stir in the remaining ingredients. Seal the lid.
4. Select the POULTRY setting, and cook for 15 minutes on High pressure.
5. Once cooking is complete, release the pressure quickly.
6. Before serving, drizzle with the remaining olive oil, and the olive rings.
7. Serve and enjoy!

Fall-Off-Bone Drumsticks

Preparation Time: 45 minutes / Servings: 3

Nutrition Facts

Per Serving: Calories 454, Carbs 6.7 g, Fiber 1.4 g, Fat 27.2 g, Protein 43.2 g

Ingredients

1 tbsp Olive Oil

6 Skinless Chicken Drumsticks

4 Garlic Cloves, smashed

½ Red Bell Pepper, diced

½ Onion, diced

2 tbsp Tomato Paste

2 cups Water

¼ cup fresh cilantro, chopped

How To

1. Heat the olive oil in your MultiPot cooker on SAUTÉ mode.
2. Add onion and bell pepper and cook for 4 minutes until the onion is translucent.
3. Add garlic and cook for a minute until it becomes golden.
4. Combine the tomato paste with water and pour it into the Pressure cooker.
5. Arrange the drumsticks inside. Seal the lid.
6. Select POULTRY and cook for 15 minutes on High pressure.
7. Once cooking is complete, release the pressure naturally for 10 minutes.
8. Sprinkle chicken with fresh cilantro.
9. Serve and enjoy!

Sweet Gingery and Garlicky Chicken Thighs

Preparation Time: 35 minutes / Servings: 4

Nutrition Facts

Per Serving: Calories 415, Carbs 21 g, Fiber 0 g, Fat 21 g, Protein 34 g

Ingredients

2 pounds Chicken Thighs

½ cup Honey

3 tsp grated Ginger

1 tbsp plus 1 tsp minced Garlic

5 tbsp Brown Sugar

2 cups Chicken Broth

½ cup plus 2 tbsp Soy Sauce

½ cup plus 2 tbsp Hoisin Sauce

4 tbsp Sriracha

2 tbsp Sesame Oil

sliced Green Onions, for garnish

How To

1. Lay the chicken in the pressure cooker.
2. Combine the remaining ingredients in a bowl.
3. Pour the mixture over the chicken. Seal the lid.
4. Select POULTRY and cook for 30 minutes on High pressure.
5. Once cooking is complete, release the pressure naturally for 10 minutes, then turn the pressure valve to release any remaining pressure.
6. Transfer chicken to a serving plate and spoon the sauce over the chicken.
7. Garnish with green onions.
8. Serve and enjoy!

Flavorful Slow-Cooked Turkey

Preparation Time: 4 hours and 15 minutes / Servings: 4

Nutrition Facts

Per Serving: Calories 487, Carbs 23 g, Fiber 1 g, Fat 28 g, Protein 47 g

Ingredients

1 Turkey Breast (enough for 4 people, about 2 pounds)

2 tsp Smoked Paprika

1 tsp Liquid Smoke

1 tbsp Mustard

3 tbsp Honey

2 Garlic Cloves, minced

4 tbsp Olive Oil

1 cup Chicken Broth

How To

1. Pat dry the turkey breast with paper towel and brush with olive oil.
2. Heat the olive oil in the pressure cooker by choosing SAUTÉ.
3. Add the turkey breast and brown it on all sides for 6 minutes.
4. Place ½ cup of chicken broth and all of the remaining ingredients in a bowl.
5. Stir to combine well. Pour the mixture over the meat.
6. Lock the lid.
7. Choose SLOW COOK mode and cook for 4 hours.
8. After 2 hours, open the lid and pour the rest of the broth inside and continue cooking.
9. Let sit for at least 5 minutes before serving. Slice the turkey breast diagonally.
10. Serve and enjoy!

Delicious Chicken Piccata

Preparation Time: 20 minutes / Servings: 6

Nutrition Facts

Per Serving: Calories 318, Carbs 12 g, Fiber 4 g, Fat 17 g, Protein 29.4 g

Ingredients

6 Chicken Breast Halves

¼ cup Olive Oil

¼ cup Freshly Squeezed Lemon Juice

1 tbsp Sherry Wine

½ cup Flour

4 Shallots, chopped

3 Garlic Cloves, crushed

¾ cup Chicken Broth

1 tsp dried Basil

2 tsp Salt

¼ cup grated Parmesan Cheese

1 tbsp Flour

¼ cup Sour Cream

1 cup Pimento Olives minced

¼ tsp White Pepper

¼ cup fresh parsley, chopped

How To

1. Dust chicken with flour.
2. Heat the olive oil in your MultiPot by setting SAUTÉ.
3. Add the chicken and cook for 6 minutes until browned on all sides, using long-handled tongs to turn. Remove the chicken from the cooker.
4. Add the shallots, and garlic and cook for a couple of minutes.
5. Add sherry, broth, lemon juice, salt, olives, basil, and pepper.
6. Return the chicken to the cooker. Seal the lid.
7. Select POULTRY and cook for 10 minutes on High pressure.
8. Once cooking is complete, release the pressure quickly
9. Carefully open the lid and transfer the chicken to a platter.
10. Add the sour cream to the cooking sauce and whisk vigorously.
11. Pour sauce over chicken and garnish with parsley.

Simple Lime Chicken with Rice

Preparation Time: 35 minutes / Servings: 4

Nutrition Facts

Per Serving: Calories 403, Carbs 44 g, Fiber 2 g, Fat 16.8 g, Protein 19 g

Ingredients

1 onion, chopped

¼ cup Lime Juice

3 tbsp Olive Oil

½ cup Salsa

2 Chicken Breasts, boneless and skinless

2 cloves garlic, minced

1 cup long-grain white rice, rinsed and drained

2 cup Chicken broth

½ tsp Pepper

½ cup Mexican Cheese Blend

½ cup Tomato Sauce

1 bay leaf

How To

1. Heat the oil in the MultiPot by setting SAUTÉ.
2. Add the onion and cook for 3 minutes until is translucent.
3. Add the garlic and saute for about 1 minute. Next, add the chicken, lime juice, tomato sauce, broth, and bay leaf and mix well.
4. Lock the lid. Select POULTRY and cook for 15 minutes on High pressure.
5. When cooking is complete, use a quick release.
6. Remove the chicken pieces with a slotted spoon and set aside. Remove and discard the bay leaf. Spoon ½ of the cooking liquid over the chicken.
7. Add the rice in the cooking liquid and add water as needed to equal 2 cups of liquid.
8. Lock the lid. Select POULTRY and cook for another 10 minutes on High pressure
9. When cooking is complete, do a quick release.
10. Serve rice with chicken and top with the cheese.

Creamy Italian-Style Spinach Chicken

Preparation Time: 15 minutes / Servings:4

Nutrition Facts

Per Serving: Calories 455, Carbs 3 g, Fiber 2 g, Fat 26 g, Protein 51 g

Ingredients

1 cup chopped Spinach

2 pounds Chicken Breasts, boneless and skinless, cut in half

½ cup Chicken Broth

2 Garlic Cloves, minced

2 tbsp Olive Oil

¾ cup Heavy Cream

½ cup Sun-Dried Tomatoes

2 tsp Italian Seasoning

½ cup Parmesan Chicken

½ tsp Salt

How To

1. Rub the meat with the half of oil, garlic, salt, and seasonings.
2. Heat the remaining oil in the MultiPot by selecting SAUTÉ.
3. Add the chicken and cook for 4 minutes on all sides.
4. Pour the broth in. Seal the lid in place; set the steam vent to Sealing.
5. Select PRESSURE COOKER and cook for 5 minutes on High pressure.
6. Once cooking is complete, release the pressure quickly. Carefully open the lid and add the cream.
7. Simmer for 5 minutes with the lid off, and then stir in the cheese.
8. Stir in tomatoes and spinach and cook on SAUTÉ just until the spinach wilts.
9. Serve and enjoy.

Basil Chicken Casserole with Cherry Tomato

Preparation Time: 30 minutes / Servings: 4

Nutrition Facts

Per Serving: Calories 337 Carbs 11.8 g, Fiber 2.6 g, Fat 21.4 g, Protein 27 g

Ingredients

8 small Chicken Thighs

½ cup Green Olives

1 pound Cherry Tomatoes

1 cup Water

A handful of Fresh Basil Leaves

1 ½ tsp minced Garlic

1 tsp dried Oregano

1 tbsp Olive Oil

How To

1. Heat the olive oil in MultiPot Pressure cooker on SAUTÉ mode.
2. Add the chicken and cook for 2 minutes per side until golden.
3. Place the tomatoes in a plastic bag and smash them with a meat pounder.
4. Remove the chicken from the cooker.
5. Next, add the tomatoes, garlic, water, and oregano in the MultiPot.
6. Top with the browned chicken. Seal the lid.
7. Select POULTRY and cook for 15 minutes on High pressure
8. When cooking is complete, use a quick release.
9. Top with the basil and olives and serve.

RED MEAT RECIPES

Tender Lamb Shanks Braised Under Pressure

Preparation Time: 50 minutes / Servings: 4

Nutrition Facts

Per Serving: Calories 535, Carbs 19 g, Fiber 2.9 g, Fat 37.9 g, Protein 41.7 g

Ingredients

4 Lamb Shanks

3 Carrots, sliced

2 Tomatoes, peeled and quartered

1 Garlic Clove, crushed

1 tbsp chopped Fresh Oregano

¼ cup plus 4 tsp Flour

8 tsp Olive Oil

1 Onion, chopped

¾ cup Red Wine

¼ cup Beef Broth

8 tsp Cold Water

How To

1. Place ¼ cup of the flour and the lamb shanks in a plastic bag.

2. Shake until you coat the shanks well. Discard the excess flour.

3. Heat 4 tsp of the oil in your MultiPot Pressure cooker by selecting on SAUTÉ.

4. Brown the shanks for on both sides, about 5-6 minutes. Set aside.

5. Heat the remaining olive oil and sauté the onions, garlic, and carrots for a couple of minutes. Stir in tomatoes, wine, broth, and oregano.

6. Return the shanks to the cooker. Seal the lid. Select MEAT/STEW and cook for 25 minutes on High pressure. When cooking is complete, use a quick release.

7. Whisk together the remaining flour and water.

8. Stir this mixture into the lamb sauce and cook with the lid off until it thickens.

Simple Sticky Baby Back Ribs

Preparation Time: 55 minutes / Servings: 6

Nutrition Facts

Per Serving: Calories 428.3, Carbs 16.6 g, Fiber 0.7 g, Fat 27 g, Protein 38 g

Ingredients

3 pounds Baby Beef Racks

2 tsp Olive Oil

1 cup Beer

½ tsp Salt

12 ounces Barbecue Sauce

½ tsp Onion Powder

¼ tsp Paprika

¼ tsp Garlic Powder

¼ tsp Black Pepper

How To

1. Cut the ribs into pieces. Mix together all of the spices in a small bowl.
2. Rub the spice mixture over the meat.
3. Heat the oil in your pressure cooker on SAUTÉ and brown the meat on all sides.
4. Insert the rack, arrange the ribs on top, and pour the beer over. Seal the lid.
5. Select MEAT/STEW and cook for 30 minutes on High pressure.
6. Once cooking is complete, release the pressure naturally for 10 minutes, then turn the pressure valve to release any remaining pressure.
7. Brush the barbecue sauce over the ribs.
8. Simmer with the lid off for a couple of minutes until sticky.

Beef Tips and Rice in Sauce

Preparation Time: 40 - 45 minutes / Servings: 4

Nutrition Facts

Per Serving: Calories 358, Carbs 14.1 g, Fiber 2.9 g, Fat 17.4 g, Protein 27.7 g

Ingredients

2 tsp Salt

2 pounds Sirloin Steaks, cut into pieces

2 tbsp Vegetable Oil

2 Onions, chopped

½ tsp Paprika

¼ tsp Mustard Powder

½ tsp Black Pepper

3 tbsp Flour

2 Garlic Cloves, minced

4 cups cooked Rice

10 ½ ounces Beef Consommé

How To

1. In a Ziploc bag, place flour, mustard powder, salt, pepper, and paprika.
2. Add the beef cubes and shake the bag to coat them well.
3. Heat the oil in your MultiPot Pressure cooker by choosing SAUTÉ and brown the meat on all sides.
4. Add the onions and garlic and cook for 3 minutes until are translucent.
5. Stir in the beef consommé. Seal the lid and select MEAT/STEW and cook for 25 minutes on High pressure.
6. Once cooking is complete, release the pressure naturally for 10 minutes, then turn the pressure valve to release any remaining pressure.
7. Simmer with the lid off until you reach your preferred consistency.
8. Serve over rice and enjoy.

Pork Chops with Potatoes in Worcestershire Sauce

Preparation Time: 35 minutes / Servings: 8

Nutrition Facts

Per Serving: Calories 415, Carbs 26 g, Fiber 3 g, Fat 30.5 g, Protein 28 g

Ingredients

1 Onion, diced

8 Pork Chops

¼ cup Butter

3 tbsp Worcestershire Sauce

1 cup Water

4 Potatoes, diced

Salt and Pepper, to taste

How To

1. Melt half of the butter in your pressure cooker on SAUTÉ mode.
2. Brown the pork chops on all sides, 4-5 minutes, and season with salt and pepper. Set aside.
3. Melt the rest of the butter in the MultiPot Pressure cooker.
4. Add onions and sauté for 2 minutes.
5. Stir in the potatoes, water and Worcestershire sauce.
6. Return the pork chops to the cooker, and seal the lid.
7. Press MEAT/STEW and cook for 15 minutes on High pressure.
8. Once cooking is complete, release the pressure naturally for 10 minutes, then turn the pressure valve to release any remaining pressure.
9. Serve and enjoy.

Delicious Potted Rump Steak

Preparation Time: 30 minutes / Servings: 12

Nutrition Facts

Per Serving: Calories 568, Carbs 11 g, Fiber 2.4 g, Fat 27 g, Protein 69 g

Ingredients

3 tbsp Olive Oil

3 Bay Leaves

6 pounds Rump Steak

2 cups diced Celery

1 tsp Salt

3 Onions, chopped

2 cups sliced Mushrooms

18 ounces canned Tomato Paste

8 ounces Beef Broth

1 ½ cups Dry Red Wine

How To

1. Heat the oil in your MultiPot Pressure cooker and brown the steak on all sides for 6 minutes. Add the vegetables and stir in all of the seasonings.
2. Combine the paste with the wine and broth in a bowl.
3. Add this mixture to the cooker.
4. Seal the lid. Select MEAT/STEW and cook for 35 minutes on High pressure.
5. Once cooking is complete, release the pressure naturally for 10 minutes, then turn the pressure valve to release any remaining pressure.
6. Check the meat and cook for a little bit more if you don't like the density or you want your meat overcooked.
7. Serve and enjoy.

Sloppy Joes and Coleslaw

Preparation Time: 30 - 35 minutes / Servings: 6

Nutrition Facts

Per Serving: Calories 276, Carbs 22 g, Fiber 4.5 g, Fat 11 g, Protein 23.5 g

Ingredients

1 cup chopped Tomatoes

1 Onion, chopped

1 Carrot, chopped

1 pound Ground Beef

1 Bell Pepper, chopped

½ cup Rolled Oats

4 tbsp Apple Cider Vinegar

1 tbsp Olive Oil

4 tbsp Tomato Paste

1 cup Water

2 tsp Garlic Powder

1 tbsp Worcestershire Sauce

1 ½ tsp Salt

Coleslaw

½ chopped Red Onion

1 tbsp Honey

½ head Cabbage, sliced

2 Carrots, grated

2 tbsp Apple Cider Vinegar

1 tbsp Dijon Mustard

How To

1. Heat the olive oil in your pressure cooker press to SAUTÉ mode and brown the meat for 4 to 5 minutes
2. Add onions, carrots, pepper, garlic powder, and salt, and sauté in hot oil until soft, 2 to 3 minutes. Stir in tomatoes, vinegar, Worcestershire sauce, water, and tomato paste. When starting to boil, stir in the oats. Seal the lid.
3. Select MEAT/STEW and cook for 15 minutes on High pressure
4. When cooking completed, release the pressure quickly and simmer with the lid off until thickened to your liking. Mix all of the slaw ingredients in a large bowl.
5. Serve the sloppy joes with the slaw.

Shredded Beef the Caribbean Way

Preparation Time: 1 hour / Servings: 4

Nutrition Facts

Per Serving: Calories 739, Carbs 2 g, Fiber 0 g, Fat 46.7 g, Protein 46 g

Ingredients

2 pounds Beef Roast

½ tsp Turmeric

1 tsp grated Ginger

4 Whole Cloves

1 tsp dried Thyme

1 tsp Garlic Powder

How To

1. Combine the turmeric, garlic, thyme, and ginger in a small bowl.
2. Rub the mixture into the beef. Stick the cloves into the beef roast.
3. Place the beer inside your MultiPot cooker and pour the ¼ cup of water around it.
4. Cook on High Pressure for about 50 minutes on MEAT/STEW.
5. When cooking completed, release the pressure quickly.
6. Shred the meat with a fork. Serve and enjoy!.

Meatballs in Creamy Sauce

Preparation Time: 25 minutes / Servings: 4

Nutrition Facts

Per Serving: Calories 608, Carbs 17 g, Fiber 2 g, Fat 37.9 g, Protein 51 g

Ingredients

½ cup Milk

1 Onion, minced

1 ½ tbsp dried Thyme

1 pound Ground Beef

1 tbsp dried Oregano

8 ounces ground Pork

¼ cup Flour

½ tsp Salt

1 slice Bread

14 ounces Chicken Stock mixed with 14 ounces Water

1 Egg

¼ cup Butter

½ cup Whipping Cream

Cooked Egg Noodles (for serving)

How To

1. Soak the bread in the milk in a bowl.
2. Add beef and pork and mix with your hands.
3. Stir in onion, thyme, oregano, egg, and salt.
4. Form ¾-inch balls out of the mixture.
5. Melt the butter in your MultiPot Pressure cooker press to SAUTÉ.
6. Whisk in the flour and gradually add the diluted chicken broth.
7. When the mixture begins to simmer, add the meatballs.
8. Seal the lid and cook on MEAT/STEW for 10 minutes on High pressure.
9. When cooking is completed, release the pressure quickly.
10. Stir in the cream and simmer with the lid off until the sauce thickens.
11. Serve over cooked noodles and enjoy.

Ginger-Flavored and Sweet Pork Belly

Preparation Time: 1 hour / Servings: 8

Nutrition Facts

Per Serving: Calories 610, Carbs 5 g, Fiber 0 g, Fat 55 g, Protein 15 g

Ingredients

2 pounds Pork Belly, cut into pieces

1 tbsp Blackstrap Molasses

2 tbsp Coconut Aminos

3 tbsp Sherry wine (or any sweet wine)

½ cup Water

2 tbsp Maple Syrup

1-inch Piece of Ginger, smashed

A pinch of Sea Salt

Freshly ground black pepper

2 scallions, chopped

How To

1. Pour the water in your pressure cooker, press SAUTÉ mode, and bring it to a boil.
2. Add the meat and let boil for 3 minutes. Drain and rinse with cold water.
3. Return the pork to the MultiPot cooker and stir in the maple syrup.
4. Brown for about 10 minutes. Stir in the remaining ingredients.
5. Seal the lid and cook on MEAT/STEW for 30 minutes on High pressure.
6. Once cooking is complete, release the pressure naturally for 10 minutes, then turn the pressure valve to release any remaining pressure.
7. Serve topped with scallions and season with black pepper.

Pot Roast in Peach Sauce

Preparation Time: 1 hour and 10 minutes / Servings: 8

Nutrition Facts

Per Serving: Calories 531, Carbs 21.6 g, Fiber 1 g, Fat 20.4 g, Protein 61.4 g

Ingredients

4 pounds Beef Roast

1 Onion, peeled and quartered

3 ½ tbsp Cornstarch

1 ½ quarts Peach Juice

3 ounces Cold Water

2 Garlic Cloves, minced

2 tbsp Olive Oil

Salt and Pepper, to taste

1 tbsp chopped fresh Parsley

How To

1. Heat the olive oil in your MultyPot Pressure cooker; press to SAUTÉ.
2. Add the pot roast and brown on all sides for 4 to 5 minutes.
3. Add the onions and garlic and cook for 2 minutes.
4. Cover the pot roast with the peach juice (add a little bit more juice if needed).
5. Seal the lid. Select MEAT/STEW and cook for 45 minutes on High pressure.
6. Once cooking is complete, release the pressure naturally for 10 minutes, then turn the pressure valve to release any remaining pressure.
7. Transfer the roast to a plate and leave to rest.
8. Whisk the water and cornstarch together and stir into the juice in the cooker.
9. Simmer with the lid off until the gravy thickens.
10. Slice the meat and pour the gravy over.
11. Top with parsley and serve with hot sauce.

Port Wine Garlicky Lamb

Preparation Time: 30 minutes / Servings: 4

Nutrition Facts

Per Serving: Calories 389, Carbs 4.7 g, Fiber 0.5 g, Fat 14.9 g, Protein 57.1 g

Ingredients

2 pounds Lamb Shanks

1 tbsp Olive Oil

½ cup Port Wine

1 tbsp Tomato Paste

10 Whole Garlic Cloves, peeled

½ cup Chicken Broth

1 tsp Balsamic Vinegar

½ tsp dried Rosemary

1 tbsp Butter

How To

1. Heat the oil in your MultiPot Pressure cooker and brown the lamb shanks on all sides for 5 to 6 minutes. Add the garlic and cook for 2 minutes until lightly browned.
2. Stir in the rest of the ingredients, except the butter and vinegar.
3. Seal the lid. Cook on High Pressure for 20-25 minutes (depending on your preferred density) on MEAT/STEW setting.
4. Once cooking is complete, release the pressure naturally for 10 minutes, then turn the pressure valve to release any remaining pressure.
5. Remove the lamb shanks and let the sauce boil for 5 minutes with the lid off.
6. Stir in the vinegar and butter. Serve the gravy poured over the shanks.

Veggie and Beef Brisket

Preparation Time: 1 hour and 30 minutes / Servings: 6

Nutrition Facts

Per Serving: Calories 653, Carbs 70 g, Fiber 8 g, Fat 28 g, Protein 32 g

Ingredients

2 pounds Beef Brisket

6 Red Potatoes, chopped

1 Onion, chopped

2 Bay Leaves

2 tbsp Olive Oil

2 cups chopped Carrots

3 tbsp chopped Garlic

3 tbsp Worcestershire Sauce

2 Celery Stalks, chopped

1 tbsp Knorr Demi-Glace Sauce

2 cups beef stock

¾ cup dry Red Wine

How To

1. Heat 1 tbsp oil in your pressure cooker on SAUTÉ mode. Cook the onion for 3 minutes until is caramelized. Transfer to a bowl. Season with salt and pepper.

2. Heat the remaining oil and cook the meat until browned on all sides for 5 to 6 minutes. Add the stock, red wine and bay leaves. Lock the lid. Cook on High Pressure for one 1 hour on POULTRY setting.

3. When cooking completed, release the pressure quickly. Add the veggies. Seal the lid and cook for another 15 minutes. Remove the bay leaves. Transfer the meat and veggies to a serving platter.

4. Whisk in the Knorr Demi-Glace sauce and simmer for 5 minutes without the lid, until thickened. Pour the gravy over the meat and serve warm.

Smokey Pork Roast

Preparation Time: 1 hour and 15 minutes / Servings: 4

Nutrition Facts

Per Serving: Calories 654, Carbs 4 g, Fiber 0.5 g, Fat 41.9 g, Protein 57.4 g

Ingredients

2 pounds Shoulder Pork

1 tsp Oregano

1 tsp Cumin

1 tsp Liquid Smoke

1 tsp Coconut Sugar

½ tsp Pepper

1 tbsp Coconut Oil

1 tsp ground Ginger

½ cup Beef Broth

1 tsp Paprika

How To

1. Place all of the spices in a small bowl and stir to combine.
2. Rub the meat with the spice mixture.
3. Melt the coconut oil in your pressure cooker on SAUTÉ setting.
4. Add the pork and cook until browned on all sides for 5 to 6 minutes.
5. Combine the liquid smoke and broth and pour over the pork.
6. Seal the lid and cook on High Pressure for about 45-50 minutes on MEAT/STEW.
7. Once cooking is complete, select Cancel and use a natural release for 15 minutes.
8. Transfer the meat to a plate and cut the pork into pieces, trimming off and discarding any extra fat. Pour the juices from the roasting over the pork.
9. Serve warm.

Beef with Cabbage, Potatoes and Carrots

Preparation Time: 1 hour and 5 minutes / Servings: 8

Nutrition Facts

Per Serving: Calories 565, Carbs 56 g, Fiber 10.7 g, Fat 21.4 g, Protein 31.6 g

Ingredients

6 Potatoes, peeled and quartered

4 Carrots, cut into pieces

2 ½ pounds Beef Brisket

1 Cabbage Head

3 Garlic Cloves, quartered

3 Turnips, chopped

2 Bay Leaves

4 cups of Water

How To

1. Pour the water into your MultiPot Pressure cooker.
2. Add the Beef, garlic and bay leaves.
3. Seal the lid and cook on High Pressure for 45 minutes on MEAT/STEW.
4. When cooking completed, release the pressure quickly.
5. Transfer the meat to a plate and cut the pork into pieces, trimming off and discarding any extra fat. Remove the bay leaves.
6. Pour the juices from the roasting over the pork.
7. Add the veggies. Seal the lid and cook for a further 5 minutes.
8. Serve immediately.

Beef and Cheese Taco Pie

Preparation Time: 20 minutes / Servings: 6

Nutrition Facts

Per Serving: Calories 413, Carbs 13 g, Fiber 6 g, Fat 26 g, Protein 35 g

Ingredients

1 package Corn Tortillas (6 pieces)

1 packet of Taco Seasoning

1 pound Ground Beef

12 ounces Mexican Cheese Blend

¼ cup Refried Beans

1 cup Water

2 tbsp Cilantro leaves

How To

1. Pour the water in your MultiPot Pressure cooker.
2. Combine the meat with the seasoning.
3. Place one tortilla into the bottom of a baking pan and place it in your cooker.
4. Top with beans, beef, and cheese. Top with another tortilla.
5. Repeat the process until you use up all of the ingredients. The final layer should be a tortilla. Seal the lid.
6. Cook on High Pressure for 12 minutes on MEAT/STEW mode.
7. When cooking completed, release the pressure quickly.
8. Remove the pan from the pressure cooker.
9. Let to cool and serve topped with cilantro.

Herbed Lamb Roast with Potatoes

Preparation Time: 30 minutes / Servings: 6

Nutrition Facts

Per Serving: Calories 494, Carbs 31.5 g, Fiber 4.2 g, Fat 16.7 g, Protein 48.9 g

Ingredients

3 pounds Leg of Lamb

1 tsp dried Sage

1 tsp dried Marjoram

1 Bay Leaf

1 tsp dried Thyme

3 Garlic Cloves, minced

2 pounds Potatoes, cut into pieces

2 tbsp Olive Oil

3 tbsp Arrowroot Powder

½ cup Water

2 cups Vegetable Broth

Salt and Pepper, to taste

Fresh cilantro, for garnish

How To

1. Heat the oil in your pressure cooker on SAUTÉ setting.
2. Combine the herbs with some salt and pepper and rub the mixture into the meat.
3. Brown the lamb on all sides for 5 to 6 minutes. Pour the broth around the meat.
4. Add in garlic and bay leaf. Lock the lid. Cook on High Pressure for 60 minutes on MEAT/STEW.
5. When cooking completed, select Cancel and release the pressure quickly. Remove the bay leaf and add the potatoes. Lock the lid and cook for a further 10 minutes.
6. Next, using a slotted spoon, transfer the potatoes and meat to a serving platter.
7. Combine the water and arrowroot and stir the mixture into the pot sauce.
8. Pour the gravy over the meat and potatoes.
9. Top with fresh cilantro and serve.

SEAFOOD RECIPES

Clams in White Wine

Preparation Time: 17 minutes / Servings: 6

Nutrition Facts

Per Serving: Calories 291, Carbs 12.8 g, Fiber 0.1 g, Fat 11.6 g, Protein 25.6 g

Ingredients

¼ cup White Wine

2 cups Fish Broth

¼ cup chopped Basil

¼ cup Olive Oil

2 ½ pounds Clams

2 tbsp Lemon Juice

2 Garlic Cloves, minced

4 Lemon Wedges

2 tbsp finely chopped fresh Parsley for garnish

How To

1. Heat the olive oil in your pressure cooker. Add garlic and cook for one minute.
2. Add wine, basil, lemon juice, and veggie broth. Bring the mixture to a boil and boil for one minute. Add your steaming basket, and place the clams inside.
3. Seal the lid and cook on High Pressure for 5 minutes on PRESSURE COOK.
4. Once finished, allow pressure to release naturally for 10 minutes, then set the steam vent to Venting to quick-release remaining pressure.
5. Check the clams and discard any unopened clams. Transfer cooked clams with cooking juices to a serving bowl.
6. Sprinkle with parsley, garnish with lemon wedges and serve.

Almond-Crusted Tilapia

Preparation Time: 10 minutes / Servings: 4

Nutrition Facts

Per Serving: Calories 223, Carbs 4 g, Fiber 2.8 g, Fat 15.6 g, Protein 28.9 g

Ingredients

4 Tilapia Fillets

1 cup sliced Almonds

1 cup Water

2 tbsp Dijon Mustard

1 tsp Olive Oil

¼ tsp Freshly ground Black pepper

Sea Salt, to taste

4 Lemon Wedges

How To

1. Pour the water in your MultiPot Pressure cooker.
2. Mix the olive oil, pepper, and mustard in a small bowl.
3. Brush the fish fillets with the mustardy mixture on all sides.
4. Coat the fish in almonds slices.
5. Place the rack in your pressure cooker and arrange the fish fillets on it.
6. Lock the lid in place; steam vent to Sealing.
7. Cook on High Pressure for 5 minutes on PRESSURE COOK setting (maybe more time if the fillets are thicker).
8. When cooking completed, do a quick pressure release.
9. Transfer the tilapia to a serving plate, and garnish with parsley and lemon wedges.
10. Serve and enjoy.

Shrimp and Egg Risotto

Preparation Time: 40 minutes / Servings: 6

Nutrition Facts

Per Serving: Calories 349, Carbs 30 g, Fiber 5 g, Fat 20 g, Protein 23 g

Ingredients

4 cups chicken broth, plus more if needed

¼ cup dry white wine

4 Garlic Cloves, minced

2 Eggs, beaten

½ tsp grated Ginger

3 tbsp Sesame Oil

¼ tsp Cayenne Pepper

1 ½ cups frozen Peas

2 cups Arborio rice

¼ cup Soy Sauce

1 cup chopped Onion

12 ounces peeled and pre-cooked Shrimp, thawed

Zest of 1 large lemon

Lemon juice from 1 lemon

1 cup finely chopped Parsley leaves

How To

1. Heat half of the olive oil in your Pressure cooker set to SAUTÉ mode.
2. Scramble the eggs and transfer to a plate.
3. Heat the remaining oil and cook the onions until tender, about 2 minutes; add the garlic and cook until aromatic, 30 seconds.
4. Stir in the remaining ingredients except for the shrimp. Seal the lid.
5. Cook on High Pressure on RICE setting for 20 minutes.
6. When cooking completed, wait about 10 minutes before doing a quick release.
7. Taste the rice and add additional broth if needed. Stir in the shrimp and scrambled eggs.
8. Let them cook for a couple of seconds until the risotto is creamy with the lid off.
9. Spoon the risotto into 6 shallow soup bowls and sprinkle with the parsley.

Lobster and Gruyere Pasta

Preparation Time: 25 minutes / Servings: 4

Nutrition Facts

Per Serving: Calories 449, Carbs 44 g, Fiber 5 g, Fat 19 g, Protein 28 g

Ingredients

6 cups Water

1 tbsp Flour

8 ounces dried Ziti

1 cup heavy cream

1 tbsp chopped Tarragon

¾ cup Gruyere Cheese

3 Lobster Tails (about 6 ounces each)

½ cup White Wine

Salt and Pepper, to taste

1 tbsp Worcestershire Sauce

1 tbsp chives, chopped for garnish

How To

1. Pour the water in the Pressure cooker. Add the ziti. Seal the lid.
2. Cook on High Pressure for 10 minutes on PRESSURE COOK.
3. When cooking completed, do a quick pressure release.
4. Drain the pasta well and set aside.
5. Place the Lobster Tails in the pressure cooker, seal the lid and cook on High Pressure for another 10 minutes on PRESSURE COOK setting.
6. Once cooked, do a quick pressure release. Remove the meat from the pot, chop it, and stir into the bowl with pasta.
7. Stir in the rest of the ingredients in pressure cooker and cook them with the lid off until the sauce thickens. Add the pasta and lobster and cook for another 1-2 minutes. Serve with chives on top.

Tuna and Peas Cheesy Noodles

Preparation Time: 17 minutes / Servings: 4

Nutrition Facts

Per Serving: Calories 384, Carbs 52 g, Fiber 4 g, Fat 9 g, Protein 21 g

Ingredients

1 can Tuna, drained

3 cups Water

4 ounces Cheddar Cheese, grated

16 ounces Egg Noodles

¼ cup Breadcrumbs

1 cup Frozen Peas

28 ounces canned Mushroom Soup

Freshly Ground Pepper to taste

Kosher salt to taste

How To

1. Place the water, mushroom soup, and noodles in your pressure cooker.
2. Seal the lid and cook on High Pressure for 5 minutes on POULTRY mode.
3. Once cooked, release the pressure quickly.
4. Stir in the tuna and frozen peas.
5. Transfer to a baking dish that can fit in your pressure cooker.
6. Toss with breadcrumbs and cheese; season with salt and pepper.
7. Place the baking dish in your MultiPot, close the lid, and cook on High pressure on PRESSURE COOK for another 3 minutes.
8. Once cooked, do a quick pressure release.
9. Serve and enjoy!

Scallops & Mussels Cauliflower Paella

Preparation Time: 17 minutes / Servings: 4

Nutrition Facts

Per Serving: Calories 200, Carbs 14 g, Fiber 3.7 g, Fat 7 g, Protein 22 g

Ingredients

2 Bell Peppers, diced

1 tbsp Coconut Oil

1 cup of Scallops

2 cups Mussels

1 Onion, diced

2 cups ground Cauliflower

2 cups Fish Stock

A pinch of Saffron

Parsley for garnish

How To

1.   Melt the coconut oil in your pressure cooker.
2.   Add onions and bell peppers and cook for about 4 minutes on SAUTÉ.
3.   Stir in scallops and saffron and cook for another 2 minutes.
4.   Stir in the remaining ingredients and seal the lid.
5.   Cook on High Pressure for 6 minutes on PRESSURE COOK.
6.   Once time is up, release the pressure naturally for 10 minutes, then turn the pressure valve to release any remaining pressure.
7.   Garnish with parsley.
8.   Serve and enjoy!

Wrapped Fish and Potatoes

Preparation Time: 15 minutes / Servings:4

Nutrition Facts

Per Serving: Calories 720, Carbs 33.3 g, Fiber 4.1 g, Fat 59.6 g, Protein 84.7 g

Ingredients

4 Salmon Fillets

4 Thyme Sprigs

2 Medium Potatoes, sliced

1 Lemon, sliced thinly

1 Onion, sliced

A handful of fresh Parsley, to garnish

2 cups of Water

2 tbsp Olive Oil

How To

1. Place each fish fillet onto a parchment paper. Divide the potatoes, thyme, onion, and lemon between the 4 parchment papers.
2. Drizzle each of them with ½ tbsp of olive oil and mix with your hands to coat everything. Wrap the fish with the parchment paper.
3. Wrap each of the 'packets' in aluminum foil. Pour the water in your pressure cooker. Place the packets inside.
4. Seal the lid and cook on High Pressure for about 5 minutes on PRESSURE COOK.
5. Once cooked, do a quick pressure release.
6. Using a large metal spatula, transfer the foil packets to plates and serve garnished with fresh parsley.

Lemony Salmon in Sauce

Preparation Time: 10 minutes / Servings: 4

Nutrition Facts

Per Serving: Calories 685, Carbs 21 g, Fiber 3.7 g, Fat 58.5 g, Protein 81.2 g

Ingredients

4 Salmon Fillets

1 tbsp Honey

½ tsp Cumin

1 tbsp Hot Water

1 tbsp Olive Oil

1 tsp Smoked Paprika

1 tbsp chopped Fresh Parsley

¼ cup Lemon Juice

1 cup of Water

1 tbsp chopped fresh Dill (optional)

How To

1. Pour the water into your MultiPot pressure cooker. Place the salmon fillets on the rack.
2. Lock the lid and cook on High Pressure for about 3 minutes on PRESSURE COOK.
3. Once cooked, do a quick pressure release.
4. Whisk together the remaining ingredients except for the dill. Drizzle the mixture over the salmon. Lock the lid and cook on High Pressure for a further 2 minutes.
5. Once cooked, do a quick pressure release.
6. Top with fresh dill (if using) and serve.

Creamy Crabmeat

Preparation Time: 12 minutes / Servings: 4

Nutrition Facts

Per Serving: Calories 305, Carbs 5.1 g, Fiber 1.1 g, Fat 16.4 g, Protein 31.8 g

Ingredients

¼ cup Butter

1 small Red Onion, chopped

1 pound Lump Crabmeat

½ Celery Stalk, chopped

½ cup Heavy Cream

¼ cup Chicken Broth

Salt and Pepper, to taste

A handful Parsley leaves, chopped

Zest of 1 lemon

How To

1. Season the crabmeat with salt and pepper to taste.
2. Melt the butter in your pressure cooker on SAUTÉ setting.
3. Add celery and cook for a minute.
4. Afterwards, add onions and cook for 3 more minutes until is soft.
5. Stir in the crabmeat and pour the broth.
6. Seal the lid and cook on High Pressure for 5 minutes on POULTRY.
7. Once cooked, do a quick pressure release.
8. Carefully open the lid and stir in the cream.
9. Serve the crabmeat on a platter sprinkled with parsley and lemon zest.

Cod in a Tomato Sauce

Preparation Time: 15 minutes / Servings:4

Nutrition Facts

Per Serving: Calories 145, Carbs 11.3 g, Fiber 1 g, Fat 2.2 g, Protein 18.8 g

Ingredients

4 Skinless Cod Fillets (about 7-ounce each)

2 cups Cherry Tomatoes, quartered

1 cup of Water

1 tbsp Extra-Virgin Olive Oil

Kosher salt and freshly ground black pepper, to taste

¼ tsp Garlic Powder

1 tbsp Thyme

2 tbsp chopped fresh Basil leaves

How To

1. Place the tomatoes in a baking dish and crush them with a fork.
2. Season the cod fillets with the thyme, garlic powder, salt and pepper and place it over the tomatoes.
3. Drizzle the olive oil. Insert the dish in your pressure cooker.
4. Close the lid and cook on High Pressure on PRESSURE COOK for 10 minutes.
5. Once cooked, do a quick pressure release.
6. Serve immediately topped with basil.

Mediterranean Salmon

Preparation Time: 15 minutes / Servings: 4

Nutrition Facts

Per Serving: Calories 693, Carbs 16.3 g, Fiber 2.7 g, Fat 56.5 g, Protein 82.9 g

Ingredients

4 Salmon Fillets

2 tbsp cup Extra-Virgin Olive Oil

1 Rosemary Sprig

1 cup Cherry Tomatoes

15 ounces Asparagus spears, trim and cut off the woody ends

1 cup Water

½ Sea Salt

½ tbsp freshly ground Black pepper

8 Lemon slices (about 2 lemons)

How To

1. Pour the water in your Pressure cooker and insert the rack.
2. Lower the salmon onto the rack, top each piece of salmon with rosemary and asparagus spears. Season with salt and pepper.
3. Seal the lid and cook on High Pressure on POULTRY for 4 - 5 minutes.
4. Once finished, release the pressure naturally for 10 minutes, then turn the pressure valve to release any remaining pressure.
5. Add the cherry tomatoes on top and cook for 1 more minute with lid off.
6. Serve drizzled with olive oil and lemon slices.

VEGETARIAN RECIPES

Meatless Shepherd's Pie

Preparation Time: 17 minutes / Servings: 4

Nutrition Facts

Per Serving: Calories 155, Carbs 22.8 g, Fiber 4.1 g, Fat 4.6 g, Protein 4.6 g

Ingredients

¼ cup diced Celery

1 cup diced Onion

2 cups steamed and mashed Cauliflower

1 tbsp Olive Oil

½ cup diced Turnip

2 cups Veggie Broth

1 cup diced Tomatoes

1 cup grated Potatoes

½ cup diced Carrot

How To

1. Heat the olive oil in your pressure cooker on SAUTÉ setting. Add onions, carrots, and celery, and cook for 5 minutes. Stir in turnips, potatoes, and veggie broth.
2. Seal the lid and cook on High Pressure for 10 minutes on PRESSURE COOK.
3. Once finished, do a quick pressure release. Stir in tomatoes. Divide the mixture between 4 ramekins. Top each ramekin with ½ cup of mashed cauliflower.
4. Pour half cup of water into your pressure cooker and set trivet inside. Lower the ramekins onto the trivet. Seal the lid and cook on High Pressure for 5 minutes on PRESSURE COOK.
5. Once finished, do a quick pressure release. Serve warm and enjoy!

Vegetarian Spaghetti Bolognese

Preparation Time: 25 minutes / Servings: 8

Nutrition Facts

Per Serving: Calories 282, Carbs 53 g, Fiber 12.2 g, Fat 3.3 g, Protein 12.1 g

Ingredients

8 cups cooked Spaghetti

1 cup Cauliflower Florets

2 cups Shredded carrots

6 Garlic Cloves, minced

2 tbsp Tomato Paste

2 tbsp Agave Nectar

1 ½ tbsp dried Oregano

56 ounces canned crushed Tomatoes

2 tbsp Balsamic Vinegar

1 tbsp dried Basil

10 ounces White Mushrooms, sliced

2 cups chopped Eggplant

1 cup Water

1 ½ tsp dried Rosemary

2 tbsp chopped fresh basil leaves

½ cup Parmigiano-Reggiano cheese, grated

How To

1. Add cauliflower, mushrooms, eggplant, and carrots to a food processor and process until finely ground. Add them to your pressure cooker.
2. Stir in the rest of the ingredients, except for the spaghetti and cheese.
3. Seal the lid and cook on High Pressure for 8 minutes on PRESSURE COOK.
4. Once cooked, do a quick pressure release. Serve the sauce over spaghetti and top with the cheese and basil.

Classic Ratatouille

Preparation Time: 20 minutes / Servings: 4

Nutrition Facts

Per Serving: Calories 104, Carbs 10.4 g, Fiber 4.5 g, Fat 7.2 g, Protein 1.5 g

Ingredients

1 Zucchini, sliced

2 Tomatoes, sliced

1 tbsp Balsamic Vinegar

1 Eggplant, sliced

1 Onion, sliced

1 tbsp dried Thyme

2 tbsp Olive Oil

2 Garlic Cloves, minced

1 cup Water

1 tbsp chopped fresh parsley

How To

1. Add the garlic in a springform pan. Arrange the veggies in a circle.
2. Sprinkle them with thyme and drizzle with olive oil.
3. Pour the water in your pressure cooker.
4. Lower the pan on trivet.
5. Lock the lid in place and set the steam vent to Sealing.
6. Cook on High Pressure for 10 minutes on PRESSURE COOK.
7. Once, finished, allow pressure to release naturally for 10 minutes, then set the steam vent to Venting to quick-release remaining pressure.
8. Top with parsley and serve.

Potato Chili

Preparation Time: 30 minutes / Servings: 4

Nutrition Facts

Per Serving: Calories 190, Carbs 22 g, Fiber 8 g, Fat 9 g, Protein 8.7 g

Ingredients

15 ounces canned Black Beans

2 cups Veggie Broth

28 ounces canned diced Tomatoes

15 ounces canned Kidney Beans

1 Sweet Potato, chopped

1 Red Onion, chopped

1 Red Bell Pepper, chopped

1 Green Bell Pepper, chopped

1 tbsp Olive Oil

1 tbsp Chili Powder

¼ tsp Cinnamon

1 tsp Cumin

2 tsp Cocoa Powder

1 tsp Cayenne Pepper

How To

1. Heat the olive oil in your pressure cooker on SAUTÉ. Add onions, peppers, and potatoes. Cook until the onions become translucent.
2. Stir in the rest of the ingredients. Seal the lid and cook on High Pressure on PRESSURE COOK for 12 minutes.
3. Once, finished, allow pressure to release naturally for 10 minutes, then set the steam vent to Venting to quick-release remaining pressure.
4. Serve warm and enjoy!

Veggie Burger Patties

Preparation Time: 30 minutes / Servings: 4

Nutrition Facts

Per Serving: Calories 115, Carbs 9.3 g, Fiber 3.5 g, Fat 7.1 g, Protein 3.4 g

Ingredients

1 Zucchini, peeled and grated

3 cups Cauliflower Florets

1 Carrot, grated

1 cup Veggie Broth

2 cups Broccoli Florets

½ Onion, diced

½ tsp Turmeric Powder

2 tbsp Olive Oil

2 cups Sweet Potato cubes

¼ tsp Black Pepper

How To

1. Heat one tablespoon oil in your pressure cooker set to SAUTÉ. Add the onions and sauté them for 3 minutes until is translucent.
2. Add the carrots and cook for an additional minute. Add potatoes and broth.
3. Seal the lid and cook on High Pressure on POULTRY mode for 10 minutes.
4. Once cooked, release the pressure quickly.
5. Stir in the remaining veggies. Seal the lid and cook on High Pressure for another 3 minutes on POULTRY mode.
6. Once cooked, release the pressure quickly.
7. Mash the veggies with a masher and stir in the seasonings.
8. Let cool for a few minutes and make burger patties out of the mixture.
9. Heat the rest of the oil in the pressure cooker set to SAUTÉ. Cook the patties for about a minute on each side.

Spicy Moong Beans

Preparation Time: 40 minutes / Servings: 8

Nutrition Facts

Per Serving: Calories 355, Carbs 62.4 g, Fiber 18.3 g, Fat 4.8 g, Protein 21.6 g

Ingredients

1 tsp Paprika

2 tsp Curry Powder

4 cups Moong Beans, soaked and drained

1 Onion, diced

Juice of 1 Lime

1 Jalapeno Pepper, chopped

1 Sprig Curry Leaves

4 Garlic Cloves, minced

2 tbsp Olive Oil

1 ½ tsp Cumin Seeds

2 Tomatoes, chopped

1-inch piece of Ginger, grated

How To

1. Heat the oil in your pressure cooker set to SAUTÉ. Add the cumin seeds and sauté for about a minute. Add onion and garlic followed by curry, ginger, and some salt. Cook for 3 minutes.
2. Stir in jalapeno, and tomatoes and cook for a further 5 minutes until soft.
3. Add the beans and pour water to cover the ingredients. Cover by at least 2 inches.
4. Add the lime juice and curry leaves and seal the lid. Cook on High Pressure for 15 minutes on PRESSURE COOK mode.
5. Once, finished, allow pressure to release naturally for 10 minutes.
6. Serve topped with parsley.

Fake Mushroom Risotto the Paleo Way

Preparation Time: 30 minutes / Servings: 2

Nutrition Facts

Per Serving: Calories 90.2, Carbs 8.4 g, Fiber 2.5 g, Fat 4.1 g, Protein 3.8 g

Ingredients

1 ½ head Cauliflower

2 cups sliced Mushrooms

1 Garlic Clove, minced

1 tsp dried Basil

1 Carrot, grated

2 cups Veggie Broth

1 tbsp Olive Oil

½ Onion, diced

How To

1. Cut the cauliflower into pieces and place them in your food processor.
2. Pulse until really ground (cauliflower rice). You should obtain about 6 cups of cauliflower rice.
3. Heat the oil in your pressure cooker set to SAUTÉ.
4. Stir in the carrots and onions and sauté for 3 minutes, until the veggies are tender.
5. Add the garlic and cook for one minute. Stir in all of the remaining ingredients.
6. Seal the lid and let cook on High Pressure for 5 minutes on PRESSURE COOK.
7. Once cooked, release the pressure quickly.
8. Serve and enjoy!

Tamari Tofu with Sweet Potatoes and Broccoli

Preparation Time: 15 minutes / Servings: 4

Nutrition Facts

Per Serving: Calories 441, Carbs 22 g, Fiber 7.2 g, Fat 29 g, Protein 24 g

Ingredients

1 pound Tofu, cubed

3 Garlic Cloves, minced

2 tbsp Tamari

2 tbsp Sesame Seeds

2 tsp toasted Sesame Oil

2 tbsp Tahini

1 tbsp Rice Vinegar

½ cup Vegetable Stock

2 cups Onion slices

2 cups Broccoli Florets

1 cup diced Sweet Potato

2 tbsp Sriracha

How To

1. Heat the sesame oil in your pressure cooker on SAUTÉ mode.
2. Add onion and sweet potatoes and cook for 2 minutes.
3. Add garlic and half of the sesame seeds, and cook for a minute.
4. Stir in tamari, broth, tofu, and vinegar.
5. Seal the lid and cook on High Pressure for 3 minutes on PRESSURE COOK.
6. Once cooked, release the pressure quickly.
7. Add broccoli, and seal the lid again. Cook on High Pressure for 2 more minutes.
8. Once terminated, release the pressure quickly.
9. Stir in sriracha and tahini before serving.

Tomato Zoodles

Preparation Time: 20 minutes / Servings: 4

Nutrition Facts

Per Serving: Calories 76, Carbs 9.6 g, Fiber 2.5 g, Fat 3.8 g, Protein 2.5 g

Ingredients

4 cups Zoodles

2 Garlic Cloves, minced

1 tbsp Olive Oil

½ cup Tomato Paste

2 cups canned diced Tomatoes

2 tbsp chopped Basil

How To

1. Place the zoodles in a bowl filled with 8 cups of boiling water. After one minute, drain them and set aside.
2. Heat the oil in your Pressure cooker set to SAUTÉ. Add garlic and sauté for about a minute, just until fragrant. Add tomato paste and basil.
3. Stir in the zoodles, coating them well with the sauce.
4. Seal the lid and cook on High Pressure on PRESSURE COOK for a minute.
5. Once terminated, release the pressure quickly. Serve right away.

Bean and Rice Casserole

Preparation Time: 40 minutes / Servings: 4

Nutrition Facts

Per Serving: Calories 510, Carbs 87 g, Fiber 9 g, Fat 4 g, Protein 18.6 g

Ingredients

1 cup soaked Black Beans

5 cups Water

2 tsp Onion Powder

2 tsp Chili Powder, optional

2 cups Brown Rice

6 ounces Tomato Paste

1 tsp minced Garlic

Salt and Black pepper, to taste

How To

1. Combine all of the ingredients in your pressure cooker.
2. Choose the PRESSURE COOK setting and close the lid. Cook on High Pressure for 35 minutes.
3. Once cooked, release the pressure quickly.
4. Serve warm and enjoy!

Sweet Potato & Baby Carrot Medley

Preparation Time: 30 minutes / Servings: 4

Nutrition Facts

Per Serving: Calories 346, Carbs 64.3 g, Fiber 13 g, Fat 7.5 g, Protein 7 g

Ingredients

1 tsp dried Oregano

2 tbsp Olive Oil

½ cup Veggie Broth

1 Onion, finely chopped

2 pounds Sweet Potatoes, cubed

2 pounds Baby Carrots, halved

How To

1. Heat the olive oil in your pressure cooker on SAUTÉ.
2. Add onions and cook for 3 minutes.
3. Add the carrots and cook for 3 more minutes.
4. Add potatoes, carrots, broth, and oregano.
5. Seal the lid and cook on High Pressure for about 10 more minutes on POULTRY
6. When finished cooking, release the pressure quickly.

Leafy Green Risotto

Preparation Time: 20 minutes / Servings: 6

Nutrition Facts

Per Serving: Calories 272, Carbs 40 g, Fiber 3 g, Fat 11 g, Protein 6 g

Ingredients

3 ½ cups Veggie Broth

1 cup Spinach Leaves, packed

1 cup Kale Leaves, packed

¼ cup grated Parmesan Cheese

¼ cup diced Onion

3 tbsp Butter

2 tsp Olive Oil

1 ½ cups Arborio Rice

4 Sun-dried Tomatoes, chopped

A pinch of Nutmeg

Salt and Pepper, to taste

How To

1. Heat the olive oil in your cooker on SAUTÉ.
2. Add onions and cook for 2 minutes until is soft.
3. Add rice and cook for 3-4 minutes. Pour the broth over.
4. Lock the lid and cook on High Pressure for 6 minutes on RICE mode.
5. Once terminated, release the pressure quickly.
6. Stir in the remaining ingredients.
7. Leave for a minute or two or until the greens become wilted.
8. Serve and enjoy.

APPETIZERS RECIPES

Creamy Potato Slices with Chives

Preparation Time: 15 minutes / Servings:6

Nutrition Facts

Per Serving: Calories 168, Carbs 31 g, Fiber 3 g, Fat 3 g, Protein 4 g

Ingredients

6 Potatoes

½ cup Sour Cream

2 tbsp Potato Starch

1 tbsp chopped Chives

½ cup Milk

1 cup Chicken Broth

1 tsp Salt

A pinch of Black Pepper

How To

1. Peel and slice the potatoes. Coat them with salt, chives, and pepper.
2. Add the broth and potatoes in your pressure cooker.
3. Seal the lid and cook on High Pressure on PRESSURE COOK for 5 minutes.
4. Once terminated, release the pressure quickly.
5. Transfer to a bowl. Whisk the remaining ingredients into the cooking liquid in your Pressure cooker.
6. Cook for one minute while whisking constantly.
7. Pour the sauce over the potatoes and serve.

Buttery Parsley Corn

Preparation Time: 10 minutes / Servings: 4

Nutrition Facts

Per Serving: Calories 289, Carbs 32 g, Fiber 12 g, Fat 19 g, Protein 5 g

Ingredients

4 ears shucked Corn

6 tbsp Butter

½ tsp Salt

1 ½ cups Water

¼ tsp Sugar

2 tbsp minced Parsley

How To

1. Combine the water, salt, sugar, and ears in your pressure cooker.
2. Seal the lid and cook on High Pressure on MULTIGRAIN for 5 minutes.
3. Once terminated, release the pressure quickly. Remove the corn from the pressure cooker and set aside.
4. Melt the butter in the Pressure cooker on SAUTÉ and add parsley.
5. When fully melted, pour the parsley butter mixture over the corn and serve.

Thyme-Flavored Fries

Preparation Time: 13 minutes / Servings: 4

Nutrition Facts

Per Serving: Calories 116, Carbs 24.4 g, Fiber 3 g, Fat 1.4 g, Protein 1.8 g

Ingredients

1 pound Potatoes, cut into strips

1 tbsp dried Thyme

½ tsp Garlic Powder

1 tsp Olive Oil

1 cup Water

How To

1. Place the potatoes in a large bowl.
2. Add thyme, olive oil, and garlic, and mix to coat them well.
3. Pour the water into your pressure cooker.
4. Arrange the fries in a veggie steamer in a single layer.
5. Seal the lid and cook on High Pressure for 5 minutes MULTIGRAIN.
6. Once finished cooking, release the pressure quickly.
7. Serve and enjoy.

Kale Chips with Garlic and Lime Juice

Preparation Time: 15 minutes / Servings:4

Nutrition Facts

Per Serving: Calories 66.5, Carbs 7.7 g, Fiber 2.4 g, Fat 3.8 g, Protein 2.3 g

Ingredients

1 pound Kale

½ cup Water

3 Garlic Cloves, minced

1 tbsp Olive Oil

2 tbsp Lime Juice

How To

1. Wash the kale and remove the stems.
2. Heat the oil in your Pressure cooker on SAUTÉ mode.
3. Add garlic and cook for a minute, or just until fragrant.
4. Pack the kale well inside the cooker.
5. Seal the lid and cook on High Pressure for 5 minutes on MULTIGRAIN.
6. Once terminated, release the pressure quickly
7. Transfer to a bowl. Drizzle the lime juice over.

Hummus Under Pressure

Preparation Time: minutes / Servings: 8

Nutrition Facts

Per Serving: Calories 161, Carbs 20.2 g, Fiber 5.9 g, Fat 6.4 g, Protein 8 g

Ingredients

1 Onion, quartered

1 Bay Leaf

2 tbsp Soy Sauce

¼ cup Tahini

¾ cup Garbanzo Beans

¼ cup dried Soybeans

¼ cup chopped Parsley

1 cup Veggie Broth

Juice of 1 Lemon

2 Garlic Cloves, minced

How To

1. Add the garbanzo beans, soybeans, and broth in your MultiPot pressure cooker.
2. Pour some water over to cover them by one inch.
3. Lock the lid and set vent to seal. Cook on High Pressure for 15 – 20 minutes on PRESSURE COOK.
4. Once, finished, allow pressure to release naturally for 10 minutes, then set the steam vent to Venting to quick-release remaining pressure.
5. Drain the beans and save the cooking liquid.
6. Place the beans along with the remaining ingredients in a food processor.
7. Process until smooth.
8. Add some of the cooking liquid to make the hummus thinner, if you want to.

Deviled Eggs

Preparation Time: 20 minutes / Servings: 4

Nutrition Facts

Per Serving: Calories 140, Carbs 2.7 g, Fiber 0.2 g, Fat 11.9 g, Protein 6.4 g

Ingredients

4 Eggs

1 tsp Paprika

1 tbsp light Mayonnaise

1 tsp Dijon Mustard

1 cup Water

Smoked paprika, for garnish

How To

1. Pour water into your pressure cooker. Place steamer basket over the water.
1. Lower the eggs onto the steamer rack.
2. Seal the lid and cook on High Pressure for 6 minutes on POULTRY.
3. Once, finished, allow pressure to release naturally for 10 minutes, then set the steam vent to Venting to quick-release remaining pressure.
4. Crack egg shells and carefully peel under cold running water.
5. Slice them in half lengthwise, removing yolks.
6. Arrange the whites onto a nice serving platter.
7. Mash the yolks using a fork with mayonnaise.
8. Add the remaining ingredients.
9. Spoon the mixture into egg whites.
10. Sprinkle with paprika and serve.

Barbecue Wings

Preparation Time: 15 minutes / Servings:4

Nutrition Facts

Per Serving: Calories 141, Carbs 7 g, Fiber 0.2 g, Fat 3.3 g, Protein 19.5 g

Ingredients

12 Chicken Wings

¼ cup Barbecue Sauce

1 cup Water

1 cup chopped Chives

How To

1. Place the chicken wings and water in your Pressure cooker.
2. Seal the lid and cook on High Pressure for 10 minutes on POULTRY.
3. Once terminated, release the pressure quickly. Rinse under cold water and pat the wings dry. Place them in your MultiPot and pour the barbecue sauce over.
4. Mix with your hands to coat them well.
5. Seal the lid and cook with the lid off on all sides, until sticky.
6. Top with chopped chives and serve.

Mini Mac & Cheese

Preparation Time: 17 minutes / Servings: 4

Nutrition Facts

Per Serving: Calories 132, Carbs 15.4 g, Fiber 1.6 g, Fat 5.4 g, Protein 7 g

Ingredients

8 ounces whole-wheat Macaroni

¾ cup shredded Monterey Jack Cheese

2 cups Water

How To

1. Place the macaroni and water in your Pressure cooker. Seal the lid.
2. Press the RICE setting and cook on High Pressure for 5 minutes.
3. Once terminated, release the pressure quickly.
4. Drain the macaroni and return them to the pressure cooker.
5. Stir in the Monterey cheese and cook for 30 seconds until really well melted with the lid off.
6. Divide between 4 small bowls and serve.

Asparagus Dressed in Bacon

Preparation Time: 17 minutes / Servings: 4

Nutrition Facts

Per Serving: Calories 224, Carbs 5.8 g, Fiber 0.1 g, Fat 14.6 g, Protein 15.6 g

Ingredients

1 pound Asparagus

8 ounces of Bacon

1 cup Water

How To

1. Pour the water into your pressure cooker.
2. Cut off the ends of the asparagus.
3. Slice the bacon in enough strips to cover each asparagus spear.
4. Wrap the asparagus in bacon.
5. Arrange the wrapped asparagus on a steamer basket.
6. Place the basket inside the Pressure cooker.
7. Seal the lid and cook on High Pressure for 5 minutes on POULTRY mode.
8. Once terminated, release the pressure quickly.
9. Serve warm

Easy Street Sweet Corn

Preparation Time: 10 minutes / Servings: 6

Nutrition Facts

Per Serving: Calories 130, Carbs 16 g, Fiber 2.4 g, Fat 5 g, Protein 9 g

Ingredients

Juice of 2 Limes

1 cup grated Parmesan Cheese

6 Ears Sweet Corn

2 cups Water

6 tbsp Yogurt

½ tsp Garlic Powder

1 tsp Chili Powder, optional

How To

1. Pour the water into your Pressure cooker.
2. Place the corn in a steamer basket and inside the cooker.
3. Seal the lid and cook on High Pressure for 3 minutes on PRESSURE COOK.
4. Once, finished, allow pressure to release naturally for 10 minutes, then set the steam vent to Venting to quick-release remaining pressure.
5. Let cool for a couple of minutes.
6. Combine the remaining ingredients, except the cheese, in a bowl.
7. Remove the husks from the corn and brush them with the mixture.
8. Sprinkle the parmesan on top.

Lemony and Garlicky Potato and Turnip Dip

Preparation Time: 15 minutes plus 2 hours in the fridge / Servings: 4

Nutrition Facts

Per Serving: Calories 143, Carbs 12.3 g, Fiber 1.7 g, Fat 10.4 g, Protein 1.2 g

Ingredients

3 tbsp Olive Oil

6 Whole Garlic Cloves, peeled

2 tbsp Lemon Juice

1 Turnip, cut lengthwise

1 Sweet Potato, cut lengthwise

1 cup Water

2 tbsp Coconut Milk

How To

1. Pour the water into your Pressure cooker. Place the potato, turnip, and garlic on the rack.
2. Close the lid and cook on High Pressure for 10 minutes on PRESSURE COOK mode. Once terminated, release the pressure quickly.
3. Place the veggies in a food processor and add the remaining ingredients.
4. Process until smooth. Transfer to a container with a lid.
5. Refrigerate for about 2 hours before serving.

DESSERT RECIPES

Tiramisu Cheesecake

Preparation Time: 1 hour plus 4 hours in the fridge / Servings: 12

Nutrition Facts

Per Serving: Calories 228, Carbs 7 g, Fiber 0 g, Fat 18 g, Protein 8 g

Ingredients

1 tbsp Kahlua Liquor

1 ½ cups crushed Ladyfingers

1 tbsp granulated Espresso

1 tbsp melted Butter

16 ounces Cream Cheese, softened

8 ounces Mascarpone Cheese, softened

2 Eggs

2 tbsp Powdered Sugar

½ cup White Sugar

1 tbsp Cocoa Powder

1 tsp Vanilla Extract

How To

1. Combine the first 4 ingredients in a bowl.
2. In another bowl beat the cream cheese, mascarpone, and white sugar.
3. Gradually beat in the eggs, along with the powdered sugar and vanilla.
4. Spray a springform pan with cooking spray.
5. Press the ladyfinger crust into the bottom. Pour the filling over.
6. Cover the pan with a paper towel and then close it with aluminum foil.
7. Pour some water in your Pressure cooker and lower the trivet.
8. Place the pan inside and seal the lid. Cook on High Pressure for about 40-45 minutes on PRESSURE COOK mode. Wait for about 10 minutes before releasing the pressure quickly.
9. Allow to cool completely before refrigerating the cheesecake for 4 hours.

Full Coconut Cake

Preparation Time: 55 minutes / Servings: 4

Nutrition Facts

Per Serving: Calories 350, Carbs 17 g, Fiber 4.5 g, Fat 31.1 g, Protein 5.5 g

Ingredients

3 Eggs, yolks and whites separated

¾ cup Coconut Flour

½ tsp Coconut Extract

1 ½ cups warm Coconut Milk

½ cup Coconut Sugar

2 tbsp melted Coconut Oil

1 cup Water

2 cups grated Coconut

How To

1. Beat the whites until soft form peaks.
2. Beat in the egg yolks along with the coconut sugar.
3. Stir in coconut extract and coconut oil.
4. Gently fold in the coconut flour.
5. Line a baking dish and pour the batter inside.
6. Cover with aluminum foil.
7. Pour the water into your Pressure cooker and place the dish inside.
8. Seal the lid and cook on High Pressure for 45 minutes on PRESSURE COOK mode.
9. Once terminated, do a quick pressure release.
10. Sprinkle with grated coconut and serve.

Oatmeal Chocolate Cookies

Preparation Time: 30 minutes / Servings: 2

Nutrition Facts

Per Serving: Calories 412, Carbs 59 g, Fiber 5.1 g, Fat 11 g, Protein 6 g

Ingredients

¼ cup Whole Wheat Flour

¼ cup Oats

1 tbsp Butter

2 tbsp Sugar

½ tsp Vanilla Extract

1 tbsp Honey

2 tbsp Milk

2 tsp Coconut Oil

⅛ tsp Sea Salt

3 tbsp Chocolate Chips

How To

1. Combine all of the ingredients in a large bowl.
2. Line a baking pan with parchment paper.
3. Make lemon-sized cookies out of the mixture and flatten them onto the lined pan.
4. Add some water in your Pressure cooker and lower the trivet.
5. Add the baking pan inside. Lock the lid.
6. Cook on High Pressure for 15 minutes on POULTRY setting.
7. Once terminated, release the pressure quickly.
8. Transfer to a wire rack to cool completely.

Peanut Butter Bars

Preparation Time: 55 minutes / Servings: 6

Nutrition Facts

Per Serving: Calories 402, Carbs 56.1 g, Fiber 4.5 g, Fat 18 g, Protein 9 g

Ingredients

1 cup Flour

1 ½ cups Water

1 Egg

¼ cup powdered Peanut Butter

¼ cup Peanut Butter, softened

½ cup Butter, softened

1 cup Oats

½ cup Sugar

½ tsp Baking Soda

½ cup Brown Sugar

How To

1. Grease a springform pan and line it with parchment paper.
2. Beat together the eggs, powdered peanut butter, softened peanut butter, butter, salt, white sugar, and brown sugar. Fold in the oats, flour, and baking soda.
3. Press the batter into the pan. Cover the pan with a paper towel and then with a piece of aluminum foil. Pour the water into the pressure cooker and lower the trivet. Place the pan inside and seal the lid.
4. Cook on High Pressure for 35 minutes on POULTRY mode.
5. Once, finished, allow pressure to release naturally for 10 minutes, then set the steam vent to Venting to quick-release remaining pressure.
6. Wait for about 15 minutes before inverting onto a plate and cutting into bars.
7. Serve and enjoy!

Compote with Blueberries and Lemon Juice

Preparation Time: Active – 10 minutes, Passive – 2 hours and 40 minutes / Servings: 4

Nutrition Facts

Per Serving: Calories 65, Carbs 15.2 g, Fiber 3.9 g, Fat 0.3 g, Protein 1.2 g

Ingredients

2 cups Frozen Blueberries

2 tbsp Arrowroot or Cornstarch

¾ cups Coconut Sugar

Juice of ½ Lemon

2 tbsp Water

How To

1. Place blueberries, lemon juice, and sugar in your Pressure cooker.
2. Seal the lid and cook on High Pressure for 3 minutes on PRESSURE COOK.
3. Once terminated, release the pressure naturally for 10 minutes.
4. Meanwhile, combine the arrowroot and water.
5. Stir the mixture into the cooked blueberries and cook on SAUTÉ stirring constantly until the mixture thickens.
6. Transfer the compote to a bowl and let cool completely.
7. Refrigerate for 2 hours.

Poached Pears with Orange, Cinnamon and Ginger

Preparation Time: 20 minutes / Servings:

Nutrition Facts

Per Serving: Calories 103, Carbs 24.7 g, Fiber 5.2 g, Fat 0.6 g, Protein 1.5 g

Ingredients

4 Pears cut in half

1 tsp powdered Ginger

1 tsp Nutmeg

1 cup Orange Juice

2 tsp Cinnamon

⅓ cup Coconut Sugar

How To

1. Combine the juice and spices in your MultiPot Cooker.
2. Place the pears on the trivet.
3. Seal the lid and cook on High Pressure for 7 minutes on PRESSURE COOK.
4. Once, finished, allow pressure to release naturally for 5 minutes, then set the steam vent to Venting to quick-release remaining pressure.
5. Place the pears onto a serving plate. Pour the juice over.

Milk Dumplings in Sweet Cardamom Sauce

Preparation Time: 30 minutes / Servings: 20

Nutrition Facts

Per Serving: Calories 75, Carbs 11.7 g, Fiber 1.4 g, Fat 1.5 g, Protein 3.4 g

Ingredients

6 cups Water

2 ½ cups Sugar

3 tbsp Lime Juice

6 cups Milk

1 tsp ground Cardamom

How To

1. Place the milk in a pot inside your Pressure cooker and bring it to a boil on Sauté mode.
2. Stir in the lime juice. The solids should start to separate.
3. Pour the milk through a cheesecloth-lined colander. Drain as much liquid as you possibly can. Place the paneer on a smooth surface.
4. Form a ball and then divide it into 20 equal pieces.
5. Pour the water in your pressure cooker and bring it to a boil.
6. Add sugar and cardamom and cook until dissolved. Shape the dumplings into balls, and place them in the syrup. Seal the lid and cook on High Pressure on PRESSURE COOK for about 4-5 minutes.
7. Let cool and then refrigerate until ready to serve.

Lemon and Chocolate Bread Pudding

Preparation Time: 45 minutes / Servings: 4

Nutrition Facts

Per Serving: Calories 312, Carbs 37 g, Fiber 2.1 g, Fat 14 g, Protein 11 g

Ingredients

3 ½ cups cubed Bread

¾ cup Heavy Cream

1 tsp Butter

2 tbsp Lemon Juice

Zest of 1 Lemon

3 Eggs

3 ounces Chocolate, chopped

½ cup Milk

¼ cup plus 1 tbsp Sugar

2 cups Water

1 tsp Almond Extract

A pinch of Salt

How To

1. Pour the water in your Pressure cooker. Grease a baking dish with butter.
2. Beat the eggs along with ⅓ cup sugar.
3. Stir in cream, lemon juice, zest, extract, milk, and salt. Soak the bread for 5 minutes. Stir in the chocolate. Pour the batter into the dish.
4. Sprinkle the remaining sugar on top. Close and seal the lid.
5. Cook for on High Pressure 18 minutes on PRESSURE COOK.
6. Release the pressure naturally for 5 minutes, then set the steam vent to Venting to quick-release remaining pressure.

Vanilla and Yogurt Light Cheesecake

Preparation Time: 1 hour and 10 minutes plus 6 hours in the fridge / Servings: 8

Nutrition Facts

Per Serving: Calories 142, Carbs 7 g, Fiber 1 g, Fat 11 g, Protein 4.6 g

Ingredients

2 Eggs

¼ cup Sugar

1 ½ cups Yogurt

1 tsp Vanilla

4 ounces Cream Cheese, softened

1 ½ cups ground Graham Cracker Crumbs

4 tbsp melted Butter

1 cup Water

How To

1. Mix the butter and cracker crumbs and press the mixture into the bottom of a springform pan (preferably a 7-inch one).
2. Beat cream cheese with yogurt, vanilla, and sugar.
3. Beat in the eggs one at a time. Spread the filling on top of the crust.
4. Place the water in your Pressure cooker and lower the trivet.
5. Place the pan inside and close and seal the lid.
6. Cook on High Pressure for 35 minutes on PRESSURE COOK.
7. Release the pressure naturally for 10 minutes, then set the steam vent to Venting to quick-release remaining pressure.
8. Let cool before refrigerating it for 6 hours. Serve and enjoy.

Pressure Cooked Cherry Pie

Preparation Time: 45 minutes / Servings: 6

Nutrition Facts

Per Serving: Calories 255, Carbs 43.6 g, Fiber 4.6 g, Fat 8.2 g, Protein 4.2 g

Ingredients

1 9-inch double Pie Crust
2 cups Water
½ tsp Vanilla Extract
4 cups Cherries, pitted

¼ tsp Almond Extract
4 tbsp Quick Tapioca
1 cup Sugar
A pinch of Salt

How To

1. Pour the water into your Pressure cooker and lower the trivet.
2. Combine the cherries with tapioca, sugar, extracts, and salt.
3. Place one pie crust on the bottom of a lined springform pan.
4. Spread the filling over. Top with the other crust. Place the pan inside the MultiPot. Seal the lid and cook on High Pressure for 18 minutes on PRESSURE COOK mode. Wait 10 minutes before releasing the pressure quickly.
5. Serve and enjoy.

Crème Caramel Coconut Flan

Preparation Time: 30 minutes / Servings: 4

Nutrition Facts

Per Serving: Calories 145, Carbs 4 g, Fiber 1.2 g, Fat 12.3 g, Protein 6.3 g

Ingredients

2 Eggs
7 ounces Condensed Coconut Milk
½ cups Coconut Milk
1 ½ cups Water

½ tsp Vanilla

How To

1. Place a pan with a heavy bottom in your MultiPot.
2. Place the sugar in the pan. Cook on SAUTÉ mode until caramel is formed.
3. Divide the caramel between 4 small ramekins. Pour the water into the pressure cooker and lower the trivet.
4. Beat the rest of the ingredients together and divide them between the ramekins.
5. Cover them with aluminum foil and place in the Pressure cooker.
6. Close the lid and cook on High Pressure for 5 minutes on PRESSURE COOK mode.
7. Once, finished, allow pressure to release naturally for 5 minutes, then set the steam vent to Venting to quick-release remaining pressure.

Chocolate Molten Lava Cake

Preparation Time: 20 minutes / Servings: 4

Nutrition Facts

Per Serving: Calories 308, Carbs 48.6 g, Fiber 2.6 g, Fat 9.2 g, Protein 5.2 g

Ingredients

2 tbsp Ghee or Butter, melted

1 cup chopped Dark Chocolate, melted

6 tbsp Almond Flour

1 cup Water

1 tsp Vanilla

3 Eggs plus 1 Yolk, beaten

¾ cup Coconut Sugar

How To

1. Combine all of the ingredients, except the water, in a bowl.
2. Grease four ramekins with some cooking spray. Divide the filling between the ramekins. Pour the water in your Pressure Cooker.
3. Place the ramekins on the trivet. Close the lid and cook on High Pressure for 10 minutes on PRESSURE COOK. Do a quick pressure release and serve chilled.

The Easiest Raspberry Curd

Preparation Time: 25 minutes plus 1 hour in the fridge / Servings: 5

Nutrition Facts

Per Serving: Calories 160, Carbs 28.4 g, Fiber 4.6 g, Fat 5.8 g, Protein 2.8 g

Ingredients

12 ounces Raspberries

2 tbsp Butter

Juice of ½ Lemon

1 cup Sugar

2 Egg Yolks

How To

1. Combine the raspberries, sugar, and lemon juice in your MultiPot Cooker.
2. Seal the lid and cook on High Pressure for a 1 minute on PRESSURE COOK.
3. Release the pressure naturally for 5 minutes.
4. Then set the steam vent to Venting to quick-release remaining pressure.
5. Puree the raspberries and discard the seeds.
6. Whisk the yolks in a bowl.
7. Combine the yolks with the hot raspberry puree.
8. Pour the mixture in your Pressure Cooker.
9. Cook with the lid off for a minute on SAUTÉ mode.
10. Stir in the butter and cook for a couple more minutes, until thick.
11. Transfer to a container with a lid.
12. Refrigerate for at least an hour before serving.
13. Serve and enjoy!

A Different Pumpkin Pie

Preparation Time: 30 minutes / / Servings: 4

Nutrition Facts

Per Serving: Calories 172.2, Carbs 39.4 g, Fiber 3.6 g, Fat 2 g, Protein 2.8 g

Ingredients

1 pound Butternut Squash, diced

1 Egg

¼ cup Honey

½ cup Milk, preferably Coconut

½ tsp Cinnamon

½ tbsp Arrowroot or Cornstarch

1 cup Water

A pinch of Sea Salt

How To

1. Place the water inside your MultiPot Cooker.
2. Place the butternut squash in the basket.
3. Seal the lid and cook on High Pressure for 4 minutes on PRESSURE COOK.
4. Do a quick pressure release.
5. Whisk all of the remaining ingredients in a bowl.
6. Drain the squash well and add it to the milk mixture.
7. Pour the batter into a greased baking dish. Place it inside.
8. Close the lid and cook on High Pressure for 10 minutes on PRESSURE COOK mode.
9. Do a quick pressure release and serve slightly chilled.

34362304R00063

Made in the USA
Columbia, SC
15 November 2018